An Introduction to the Peoples and Cultures of Micronesia

Second Edition

William H. Alkire
University of Victoria, British Columbia

Cummings Publishing Company
Menlo Park, California • Reading, Massachusetts
London • Amsterdam • Don Mills, Ontario • Sydney

Preface

to the Second Edition

This book provides the first overall survey of the peoples and cultures of Micronesia since the anthropological information explosion on the area began in the 1950s. It attempts to summarize these studies in a logical and coherent fashion.

Ten island societies of Micronesia have been selected and discussed in some detail; these societies reflect a range of cultural adaptations to the varying microenvironments of the region. An attempt is made throughout to emphasize similarities in organizational patterns, where such exist, without losing sight of individuality.

The book begins with a general introduction to the geography, settlement, and initial migrations that have affected the area. The following chapters discuss the main islands or island groups of the western, central, and eastern subdivisions of the region. Specifically, the cultural patterns of the Marianas, Palau, Yap, central Caroline atolls, Truk, Ponape, Kusaie, Marshalls, Gilberts, and Nauru are provided. The emphasis is on traditional forms of adaptation, economic activities, and political organization. The final chapter (new to this edition) discusses present-day political and economic developments that are associated with the changing status of the Trust Territory of the Pacific Islands, which comprises the bulk of the Micronesian islands.

It is hoped that this book will provide a resource on Micronesia for students, teachers, and the general reader that not only conveys basic information about the area, but through its bibliography introduces the reader to the now numerous detailed studies of particular societies, institutions, and theoretical problems of the region. And finally, I hope this volume will serve to partially balance the readily available readings on Oceanian cultures, which hitherto generally have emphasized the neighboring areas of Polynesia and Melanesia.

I want to thank those readers who offered comments on the first edition and acknowledge that several changes in the text have followed from their helpful suggestions. I am indebted to Roland Force, Ward Goodenough, Robert Kiste, Bernd Lambert, Saul Riesenberg, David Schneider, and Jack Tobin for their helpful comments on various sections of an earlier draft of this book. The author alone, however, is responsible for the choices, emphases, and conclusions presented. Finally, I wish to acknowledge that the maps and illustrations in this book were prepared with the aid of a grant from the University of Victoria.

William H. Alkire
August 1976

Contents

For my parents

About the Author

William H. Alkire received his B.A. from the University of Washington, M.A. from the University of Hawaii, and Ph.D. from the University of Illinois, all in anthropology. He has conducted more than three and one-half years of field work in Micronesia, primarily on Lamotrek, Woleai, and Faraulep atolls and Saipan Island. Dr. Alkire previously held a research position at the Bishop Museum in Honolulu and teaching positions at San Francisco State University and the University of Malaya, and he is currently at the University of Victoria in British Columbia. He is the author of several articles and one other book based on his Micronesian research.

Chapter 1
Introduction

Magellan's chronicler, Antonio Pigafetta, recorded as
follows the first contact between Micronesians and Europeans:

> On Wednesday, the 6th of March (1521) we discovered
> a small island in the north-west direction, and two
> others lying to the south-west. . . . The captain
> general wished to touch at the largest of these
> three islands to get refreshments of provisions;
> but it was not possible because the people of these
> islands entered into the ships and robbed us, in
> such a way that it was impossible to preserve one-
> self from them. Whilst we were striking and lower-
> ing the sails to go ashore, they stole away with
> much address and diligence the small boat called the
> skiff, which was made fast to the poop of the cap-
> tain's ship, at which he was much irritated, and
> went on shore with forty armed men, burned forty or
> fifty houses, with several small boats, and killed
> seven men of the island; they recovered their skiff.

In the course of the 450 years that have since passed,
Micronesians from every inhabited island of the region's
four archipelagoes--the Mariana, Caroline, Marshall, and
Gilbert Islands (Map 1)--have experienced firsthand contact with foreign administrators, traders, missionaries,
or soldiers. Most subsequent encounters have been less
violent than that between Magellan and the Chamorro of
the Mariana Islands, but some have been far worse.
     Even though formal Spanish sovereignty was pro-
claimed over the Mariana Islands in 1564 and Spanish
missionaries soon after attempted--albeit unsuccessfully--

1

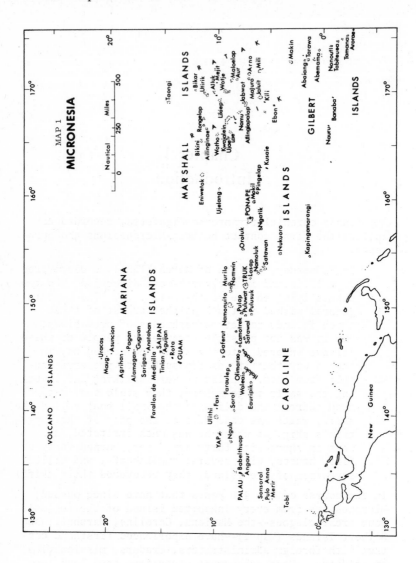

to extend their work into the Carolines, significant outside influences were not felt in Micronesia beyond the Marianas until the middle of the nineteenth century. At that time the major islands in the area began to experience frequent visits of whaling and trading vessels. By the 1880s the Spanish, German, and British governments were engaged in a series of complicated moves and countermoves, which included a British bombardment of a Palauan village in 1882, papal arbitration of disputed German and Spanish claims, and an agreement that gave Spain administrative rights and Germany commercial rights throughout most of the area. The colonial history of Micronesia since that time is outlined in Table 1.

The Marianas, Carolines, and Marshalls have since been governed by the Germans, Japanese, and Americans. Only the Gilbert Islands have experienced the relative stability of a single colonial government (interrupted by Japanese occupation during World War II). Micronesia has suffered because of its location, a location that has made it a focal point for other people's quarrels. Colonial control of the area has time and again changed because of external conflicts--the Spanish-American War (when Guam was taken by the Americans and Spain sold her remaining Micronesian possessions to Germany), World War I (when Japan displaced Germany), and World War II (when America supplanted Japan).

Life on many of the islands of Micronesia has changed significantly as a result of this contact. Today a visitor does not have to look very far to see a multitude of obviously introduced material items ranging from Japanese automobiles and motorcycles in the main port towns to sail canvas and metal cooking pots on even the most remote outer island. The social changes that have resulted are less universal, since the outside world has had little to offer in this sphere that has improved upon the traditional adaptation in the more remote areas of Micronesia. However, in those cases where even the basic parameters of sociopolitical organization have changed, the emphasis in the main body of this book remains on traditional forms and reflections of such traditional forms in contemporary life. Some aspects of modern political change are discussed in the final chapter.

TABLE 1
Periods of foreign influence in Micronesia

Period	Marianas	Carolines	Marshalls	Gilberts
Traders, whalers, freebooters	—	1840-1885	1840-1888	1840-1892
Spanish colonial administration	1564-1898	1885-1898	—	—
German colonial administration	1899-1914	1899-1914	1888-1914	—
Japanese mandate/ occupation	1914-1945	1914-1945	1914-1945	1942-1943
British colonial administration	—	—	—	1892-present
American trust territory	1945-present	1945-present	1945-present	—

THE SETTING

The more than 2000 individual islands that make up Micronesia amount to little more than 1000 square miles of land. Guam, with an area of 225 square miles, is the largest single island of the region. At the other extreme are several inhabited atoll islands--perhaps more accurately termed islets--less than 0.04 of a square mile in area. Excluding the mixed Guamanian population, these islands are at present inhabited by between 125,000 and 135,000 native Micronesians.

The islands of Micronesia are not all of a single type. The Marianas are volcanic, the Carolines include both volcanic and coral islands, while the Marshalls and Gilberts are exclusively coral formations. Volcanic or "high" islands provide an interesting contrast to "low" coral islands, for high islands are a single, continuous formation rising directly from the ocean floor and sometimes reaching elevations of several thousand feet above sea level. The volcanic activity which built such islands may be quite ancient, as in the cases of Palau and Yap, or geologically fairly recent, as in the case of Kusaie. The only area of current volcanic activity in Micronesia lies in the northern Mariana Islands.

The two major types of coral islands are atolls and raised individual islands. Both are the result of continued coral growth around or on a volcanic base. The classic atoll reef, which is circular in form, began as an offshore fringing reef surrounding a slowly subsiding volcanic island (Darwin, 1901). The reef continues to grow long after the subsiding volcanic "core island" has disappeared below sea level. Then, as a result of sea and storm erosion, deposits of detritus accumulate in protected locations along the reef. These deposits may amount to no more than a small sand dune, or they may accumulate to form an island with an average elevation of six to eight feet above sea level extending along the reef for several miles. Raised coral islands, as a type, are less common in the western Pacific. They are usually thought to have formed on a volcanic base which has reversed a pattern of subsidence so that the coral formation has been raised above sea level, perhaps as much as 50 or more feet.

There are important topographic and edaphic

differences between volcanic and coral islands which
directly influence the quantity and variety of vegetation
found on each, and this in turn determines how attractive
each may be as a home for humans. Volcanic islands are
generally larger, have a more variable topography, and
possess richer soils than coral islands; thus they almost
always have a greater variety of plants growing on them
as well as more numerous and distinct vegetation zones.
Climatic variables, of course, are of equal importance
in determining the floral characteristics of any particular island.

The tropical maritime climate of Micronesia is char-
acterized by year-round temperatures which average in the
eighties, generally high rainfall and humidity, and seasonal trade winds (November through April or May in most
areas). Rainfall is highest in a belt which stretches in
an east-west direction just north of the equator--thus
covering most of the Caroline Islands--and decreases
gradually as one moves either north or south. There is
also a marked decrease in rainfall toward the eastern end
of Micronesia. Ponape, in the central Carolines, is one
of the wettest islands of the region, receiving an annual
average of 180 inches fairly evenly distributed throughout the year. Even the low coral islands of the Carolines
average more than 100 inches per year. The northern Marianas, northern Marshalls, and southern Gilberts, on the
other hand, have the lowest yearly averages, marked seasonal variation, and periodic droughts. The northern
Marshalls and all of the Marianas average between 70 and
80 inches per year, while the southern Gilberts have less
than 40 inches. Yearly fluctuations in many of the Gilbert Islands are unpredictable. For example, Nauru, an
isolated island west of the Gilberts, may have 170 inches
in one year and less than 15 inches in the next. Such
seasonal variation and yearly fluctuations can seriously
limit the number of plant species which are able to survive on a coral island, because ground water is also
scarce and solely dependent on rainfall. If rainfall is
not high or is unevenly distributed through the year, the
Ghyben-Hertzberg water lens contained by the porous coral
substratum tends to dissipate into the surrounding salt
water.[1] (All notes appear at the end of the book.)

Rainfall is not a problem in the Caroline Islands,
but typhoons are. These severe tropical storms may ori-

ginate as far east as the southern Marshalls but more
frequently rise in the central Carolines and move westward, occasionally along the chain of islands, before
veering northwest and passing either through the southern
Marianas or near Ulithi and Yap. The high winds and salt
water carried by the winds can so severely damage vegetation that it may not recover for six or seven years. On
a coral island the magnitude of the damage can be disas-
trous; destruction is usually considerably less on the
larger volcanic islands where topography and size provide
greater shelter.

The subsistence staples cultivated in Micronesia are
generally the same on both high and low islands. Breadfruit, taro (*Colocasia, Cyrtosperma,* and *Alocasia,* which
collectively are more accurately termed aroids), coconuts, and yams (on high islands) are the most important.
Pandanus is also important on the drier coral islands of
eastern Micronesia. On a few islands sweet potatoes,
cassava (manioc), and maize (all introduced in postcontact times) are also grown. Faunal life is very limited. Pigs, chickens, and dogs (on some islands) are
eaten; it is generally agreed that pigs, and in some
areas dogs, were introduced to Micronesia by Europeans.
Traditionally on the larger islands of the Marianas and
Carolines fruit bats were hunted, and on most islands
various species of wild birds are occasionally caught and
eaten. Most of the islands have a multitude of rats and
lizards but these are not eaten. By far the most important source of protein in the diet of Micronesians comes
from the multitude of reef, lagoon, and blue-water fishes,
supplemented by shellfish and sea turtles.

The two aspects of the Micronesian environment that
seem to dominate Micronesian thought are the near-univer-
sal scarcity of land and the weather (depending on location), either in the form of droughts or typhoons. Nearly all of the peoples of Micronesia have had to adapt to
these harsh facts of the environment.

THE PEOPLE

At this time any attempt to reconstruct the original peo-
pling of Micronesia involves sifting a variety of
sources--archaeological, linguistic, ethnological, and

botanical--and even then, because of the limited amount
of archaeology that has been done in the area, one must
be satisfied with an incomplete picture. Nevertheless,
two things are clear: (1) the forebears of the Micronesians were of Asian origin (as was their inventory of
cultivated plants), and (2) the settlement of Micronesia
was not the result of a simple one-way movement of a mass
of humanity.

Most early theories of population movements in
Oceania were directly or indirectly influenced by "horde"
and "wave" thinking. Peter Buck, for example, in his
classic 1938 study of Polynesian culture history, spoke
of the hordes that "poured into Indonesia from the main-
land of Asia" (1938, p. 42). Others have referred to
waves of migrants moving from Asia into the Pacific.
Many horde and wave theorists have uncritically projected
present conditions into the past, overlooking the fact
that cultures are continually adapting to changing natural
and social environments. Buck's view of the settlement
of Polynesia and Micronesia, however, seems to have been
most limited by its emphasis on the seemingly significant
racial differences between Polynesians and Micronesians,
on the one hand, and Melanesians, on the other--an emphasis that suffered from the then limited understanding of
physical types and human genetics.

Buck based his reconstruction on a three-stock theory
of race which found it difficult to derive "Europoid"
Polynesians from "Negroid" Melanesians. He therefore
emphasized a northern migration route for the Polynesians
through Micronesia. In this reconstruction the Micronesians were seen as remnants left behind by the Polynesian ancestral migrants as they passed through the area.
The Micronesians, of course, are not identical in physical
type to the Polynesians but they were, in Buck's terms,
closer to the Polynesian type than the dark-skinned Melanesians. He thought it unfortunate, as far as the clarity
of the prehistoric record was concerned, "that the original population of Micronesia had been overlain by Mongoloid elements that crept in after the ancestors of the
Polynesians had passed through" (1938, p. 47).

Recent developments in human genetics have shown
that racial history is neither simple nor inflexible even
in small and relatively isolated populations. The range
of physical types found in most Oceanic communities is

great, and it is fairly simple in Micronesia to find
within the same village individuals whom anthropologists
of 30 years ago would have labeled "Mongoloid," "Negroid,"
and "Europoid" (or "Caucasoid"). In the majority of cases
population movements in Oceania involved small groups,
perhaps no more than one or two canoes full of individuals. Under these circumstances it is relatively easy to
derive the "Polynesian physical type" from a Melanesian
location, even if one assumes the by no means proven fact
that the "typical" Melanesian of today is identical in
physical type to the inhabitants of those islands at the
time Polynesia began to be settled. A lone canoe filled
with individuals drawn from a single locality probably
would not contain a representative cross section of the
"mother" population gene pool. If the voyagers made
landfall on an uninhabited island and remained isolated
in this new location for a number of generations, it is
quite likely that the average physical type of these
descendants would have diverged significantly from that
of the average individual in the area from which the original migrants came. R. T. Simmons and his colleagues
have succinctly summarized some of the reasons for the
highly variable genetic patterns found among Micronesians:

> This is surely the outcome of the various factors
> resulting from (1) genetic sampling in groups of
> very small size and usually covered by Sewell
> Wright's term "random genetic drift" and, perhaps
> even more importantly, from (2) historical accident
> and chance which, within these small groups, has
> time and again returned the genetic fate of the
> small communities to a few new "founders". . . .
> The vicissitudes of history (viz. typhoon, tidal
> wave, volcanic eruption, canoe sinkings, accidental
> canoe voyages, plagues, pestilence, famine and the
> ravages of warfare and vendetta, together with tran-
> sient and faddish changes in sexual practices) can,
> in such small groups, result in very few of the mem-
> bers giving rise to the succeeding generation, and
> these few represent a fortuitous, rarely any "mean or
> average," sampling from the gene pool of the commu-
> nity. (Simmons et al., 1965, p. 152)

William Howells (1974), another physical anthropologist, however, has recently revived the northern-migration-

route theory in a more complex four-phase sequence, based
primarily on his interpretation of physical anthropological
data. He suggests that Austronesian-speaking migrants
entered Micronesia about 4000 B.C. from the Philippines-
Indonesia area. These migrants established permanent
settlements only on the richer high islands. About
2000 B.C. the central volcanic islands of Micronesia--
Truk, Ponape, and Kusaie--were populated to capacity,
precipitating new movements onto the atolls of the central
Carolines and into the coral island chains of the Marshalls, Gilberts, and Ellice Islands, where the settlers
mastered a new atoll adaptation. By 1500 B.C. numbers of
these migrants were arriving in Fiji and Tonga. Continued
dispersal and language differentiation within Micronesia
occurred from 1000 B.C. to the present, with population
movements in all directions, thus complicating the culture
history of the area. The accuracy of this argument must
await some archaeological support, for at present it depends on the premise that early migrants indeed did bypass
the central Caroline atolls--some of which are rich in
resources--in favor of the high islands, as well as on a
particular interpretation of the presently known physical
anthropological and linguistic evidence, which Howells
readily admits is open to a number of interpretations.

At this time the weight of the linguistic and archaeological evidence is, in fact, increasingly pointing to
Melanesia, specifically the Fiji-New Hebrides area, as
having the most direct links not only to Polynesia but
also to a large part of eastern and central Micronesia.

The earliest settlements in Micronesia, however, were
made in the western islands and were most likely made by
drift voyagers from the Philippines and Indonesia. In
1957 Alexander Spoehr published a radiocarbon date derived
from materials obtained in his archaeological work on Saipan which indicated that the island was settled by
1500 B.C.[2] No dates of similar antiquity have been obtained outside the Marianas, the next oldest date being
A.D. 176, obtained on Yap by E. W. and D. S. Gifford. On
the basis of their analysis the Giffords concluded that
"excavations in Yap have demonstrated a close connection
between the archaeology of that island and the Marianas,
evidenced by at least two important types of ancient artifacts, potsherds and shell adzes" (1959, p. 200). The
early unlaminated plain potsherds found on Yap appear

nearly identical to the plain-ware sherds which Spoehr
found as a dominant later type in the Mariana Islands.
Furthermore the Giffords believed that the Yapese shell
adze blades more closely resembled those of Saipan than
specimens from other islands of the Carolines. No intensive archaeological work has yet been reported from Palau,
the remaining major area of western Micronesia, but Douglas Osborne in 1966 concluded (p. 464) on the basis of a
survey that Palau was settled as early as the Marianas.

Both Spoehr and Osborne see similarities in the prehistoric record between Micronesia and the Philippines,
but whereas Spoehr traces this relationship to the earliest settlers in the Marianas, Osborne emphasizes a later
date--perhaps A.D. 500--for Philippine-Palau ties and
suggests that the earliest migrants into the western
Carolines drifted there from eastern Indonesia (specifically the Halmahera-Morotai-Celebes region). It seems
quite likely that drift canoes arrived in Micronesia from
both of these areas. Similarities in artifacts also indicate that after initial settlement irregular and small-
scale movement occurred between the Marianas, Yap, and
Palau, but this contact was neither intense nor frequent,
for the communities had developed three distinct cultures
at the time of initial European contact.

Since there are no comparable archaeological data
for the rest of Micronesia that would permit a wider reconstruction, one must rely on linguistic evidence.[3] All
the languages of Micronesia belong to the Austronesian
(Malayo-Polynesian) language family (or phylum, in Isadore
Dyen's classification). Traditionally Micronesian languages were grouped in contrast to three other Oceanic
subgroups--Indonesian, Melanesian, and Polynesian. However, detailed analysis of various Micronesian languages
by several linguists has shown that such a contrast is
misleading.

To date Dyen's (1965) study of shared cognates is
the most comprehensive and it has shown that Yapese, Chamorro, and Palauan are all only distantly related to the
languages of "nuclear" Micronesia, which include Marshallese, Ponapean, Trukese, Wolean, and the slightly more
distant Gilbertese. In fact Dyen's data suggest these
latter languages are more closely related to New Hebridean, Rotuman, and Fijian than they are to Yapese, Chamorro, or Palauan--the final two in fact appear to have

closer links with certain languages of the Celebes than
to any nuclear Micronesian language.

George Grace, another linguist, using what he calls
a "historical method" that analyzes a wide range of linguistic variables, also concludes that Palauan and Chamorro (he does not specifically mention Yapese) are not
of the same "eastern Austronesian" subgroup as other
Micronesian languages--a subgroup that "has its closest
linguistic affiliations with languages of the New Hebrides" (1961, p. 364).[4] Finally, W. K. Matthews, in a
brief linguistic analysis which predates both Dyen's and
Grace's, reached a similar conclusion. His study defined
two distinct linguistic types in Micronesia, "a marginal
Indonesian type represented by the vernaculars of the
Palaus and the Marianas . . . which probably constitute
two separate branches . . . and a nuclear non-Indonesian
type, which comprises the vernaculars of the Carolines,
Marshalls, and Gilberts" (1951, p. 436). Matthews, like
the others, further suggested close links between nuclear
Micronesian and Melanesian languages--a connection he
notes was proposed by a German linguist as long ago as
1908.

In sum, then, it seems that migrants entered Micronesia from at least two different directions, first from
the Philippines and Indonesia and later from eastern Melanesia (Map 2). Descendants of those who entered from the
east ultimately established communities throughout the
Gilberts, Marshalls, eastern and central Carolines, and
eventually occupied islands as far west as Sonsoral, Pulo
Anna, Merir, and Tobi southwest of Palau (indeed, present-
day inhabitants of these islands claim descent from Ulith-
ians). Descendants of those who entered from the west
have a more limited distribution--Palau, Yap, and the
Marianas--although it should certainly be remembered that
canoes from outside Micronesia continued to arrive from
time to time in much the same fashion as the original migrants. Furthermore, as populations began to grow on
individual Micronesian islands, internal movements and
migrations increased. All of these movements, whether
purposeful or accidental, involved small groups of people
and therefore had little chance of significantly altering
the already established communities numbering in the hundreds. Nevertheless, movements of this type did serve to
diffuse ideas and material items from island to island

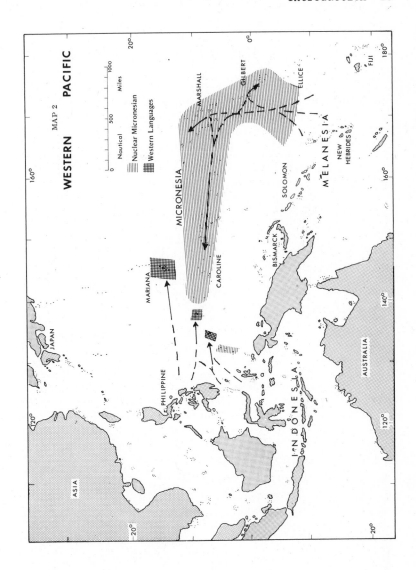

throughout nearly the whole of Micronesia.

By the time Magellan arrived in the Marianas all the major islands of Micronesia either were occupied by permanent settlers or were known and periodically exploited by one or more neighboring communities. By that time, as well, the languages of Micronesia had diverged into at least 12 distinct vernaculars. It is interesting to note that the languages with the widest geographic distribution were those associated with coral-island populations, that is, central Carolinian and Marshallese. Not only does this reflect, perhaps, a shorter period of separation, but also the intensive contact maintained between these islands of limited resources. Among Micronesians the low islanders in general had the most highly developed canoe and navigation technology, a virtual necessity for survival on such vulnerable islands. In contrast, most of the high islands of Micronesia were populated by groups speaking languages of restricted distribution and whose inhabitants rarely took their canoes beyond sight of their own coastline. In most cases, of course, there was no reason for them to do so--interisland travel had no real value for the high islander who resided in a well-protected and relatively rich environment. The two ironies of this situation were, first, that the residents of the small, so-called isolated coral islands of Micronesia were often more traveled and "worldly wise" than the inward-looking and "self-centered" residents of the large and well-known volcanic islands; and second, even in traditional times, when high islander met low islander it was the former who played the knowledgeable sophisticate and the latter the self-effacing "countryman." These contrasting roles, however, can be understood in the light of the political and population realities of the area. The high islands universally had larger populations and more reliable and abundant resources; thus both in rounds of frequent warfare (in precontact Micronesia) and in the course of normal interaction, the high islanders were in an advantageous position. Nevertheless, conquest of a neighbor's territory did not give access to an appreciably different range of material resources, only a larger quantity.

All Micronesians depended on wood, stone, coral, shell, and various fibers (pandanus, hibiscus, banana, coconut) in the manufacture of their basic material culture inventory. The differences in high- and low-island tech-

nologies were of emphasis rather than of kind. Cultivation of taro patches and breadfruit or coconut groves was
accomplished with simple wooden digging sticks, shell axes
and knives, bamboo knives, and harvesting sticks. Metal
replaced stone and shell in the eighteenth century, but
the basic inventory of subsistence tools has not increased
appreciably since the time of Magellan. Similarly, fishing equipment utilized shell hooks, sennit lines and nets,
latticework wooden traps, pole or stone weirs, and wooden
spears; all were produced with equal ease on volcanic or
coral islands.

The single outrigger canoes of the Marshallese and
Carolinians (and reported for precontact Mariana society)
were the most impressive achievement of Micronesian technology. Their carefully proportioned and finely hewn
multipiece hulls (often more than 40 feet long) were
lashed tightly together with coconut coir. Hulls were
built with a controlled asymmetry that improved maneuver-
ability when under way. They were rigged with plaited
lateen sails. These craft enabled the low islanders to
travel widely in their respective archipelagoes (Alkire,
1970; Gladwin, 1970).

Only slightly less impressive were the large meeting
houses found in the Gilberts, Palau, Yap, Ponape, and in
less elaborate forms in the central Carolines and Truk.
These buildings were rectangular with high roofs resting
on cornerposts sunk in the ground; and, with the exception
of Palau, where walls, cornerposts, and roofs were carefully mortised and fitted, ridgepoles, rafters, and plates
were held together solely with sennit lashings. Roofs
were thatched with pandanus or palm leaves. In prehistoric times large structures of this type probably occupied the artificially constructed foundation complexes in
Ponape and Kusaie (Kubary, 1885; Wilson, 1968).

Ordinary dwellings were much smaller but similarly
constructed. In the Marianas and Palau they were raised
above ground level and had plank floors. On Yap all
structures rested on raised stone platforms, while in the
rest of Micronesia they were built directly on the ground
with earth or gravel floors covered with mats. Regular-
ized proportions were maintained during construction, and
the status of the occupants might be reflected in the
construction proportions chosen (see Alkire, 1970).

House decorations were comparatively more elaborate

in the western than in the eastern islands.   Incised and
painted or lime-inlaid geometric designs, decorated
rafters, beams, and houseposts (Mason, 1964).   Palauan
motifs were the most elaborate, including figures and
scenes from traditional histories and legends (modern-day
"story boards" are descendants of the beam and gable
decorations of traditional Palau).   Nevertheless, wood
carving in the whole of Micronesia was not as elaborate
or varied as that of Melanesia.   Thilenius (1913-1938)
provides excellent illustrations of the full range of
Micronesian structures.

Micronesian household utensils were relatively simple.   Finely plaited pandanus sleeping mats and simple
coconut frond mats for casual day-to-day use were found
everywhere.   Carved wooden bowls, shell containers,
plaited baskets, and, in the Carolines, a backstrap loom
were all that cluttered the interior of the single-room
dwellings.   The cooking house, which stood apart from the
sleeping house, had a hearth, food pounders, and a coconut
grater.   In historic times only the Yapese manufactured
pottery, but in the prehistoric period pottery was also
found in Palau and the Marianas.

Early Spanish documents note that the inhabitants of
the Marianas went naked.   Clothing was found in most other
areas, however.   Carolinian men wore a loincloth woven of
banana fiber.   The technology of loom weaving diffused to
the area from Indonesia (Riesenberg and Gayton, 1952).
Women on Yap wore voluminous grass skirts.   In the rest of
the Carolines wrap-around skirts, woven in the same fashion as men's loincloths, covered a woman from the waist to
the knees.   Alternating longitudinal stripes, formed by
varying colored warp threads, were the main decorative
design in weaving, although in some instances geometric
designs were worked as brocade into the cloth.   In the
Marshalls both men and women wore plaited pandanus mats,
the men about their loins and the women from waist to
ankles.

The decorative arts in Micronesia concentrated on
personal adornment.   Necklaces, bracelets, belts, girdles,
and earrings (often worn in such numbers as to distend the
earlobe to shoulder level) were made of turtle shell, various sea shells, and polished coconut shells.   Combs and
flower garlands decorated the head.   Turmeric and coconut
oil were used as cosmetics on face, shoulders, back, and

chest. Immature coconut frond leaflets, of luminescent yellow hue, were often tied about the arms, fingers, wrists, waist, and ankles on festive occasions and during dances.

Tattooing was important in most of Micronesia. The same geometric designs incised on house rafters and beams were often seen as tattoos on arms or legs. In the central Carolines the whole of a man's torso, front and back, might be covered with symmetrical fields of a grand design--a reflection of his high status in some communities.

Chants, songs, and dances were important art forms even though most areas of Micronesia lacked musical instruments. Men of importance had songs composed by wives or sweethearts about their deeds and abilities; these songs lived on after the death of the men and tended eventually to elevate some such individuals to near "culture hero" status. The sitting and standing dances of the area were performed by groups of the same sex, and they also recounted stories and events of the present and past.

Many traditionally manufactured items have been abandoned, of course, in favor of more durable or prestigious foreign goods, and this has necessitated a shift from purely subsistence economic activities to commercial ones. Even the two most impressive examples of traditional technology--houses and canoes--are disappearing in favor of western substitutes. Missionary activities are another foreign influence that has resulted in significant changes. Roman Catholic missionaries in western Micronesia and Protestant missionaries in the eastern islands have succeeded in converting all but a very small percentage of the population. The remaining non-Christians are limited to small pockets of traditionalists in the central Carolines and Yap, and a nativistic cult group in Palau.

Traditional Micronesian religious beliefs embraced a variety of spirits and ghosts and emphasized ancestor worship in one or another form (Mason, 1968). Chamorros and Gilbertese kept the skulls of deceased ancestors, and many Carolinians had ancestral shrines in or near their dwellings. One's soul was thought to vacate the body at death, either going to an afterworld, variously conceptualized, or remaining on the island to help or harm the living. Whether a ghost was benevolent or malevolent often depended on the mode of death. A natural death potentially meant a benevolent ghost, while an unnatural death (accidental, through foul play, during pregnancy or childbirth) forecast a malevolent ghost.

Spirits whose origins were independent of people were also associated with places and natural objects, and a number of spirits were associated with special crafts and activities. Housebuilders, canoe builders, navigators, diviners, and medical practitioners all had patron spirits that controlled the outcome of their efforts and to whom chants and offerings were made. Taboos, often involving food and sexual restrictions, were placed on one's behavior for a specified period of time before, during, or after engaging in important pursuits. If the taboo were violated, the offended spirit might send sickness or death not only to the violator but to the community at large. All sickness was caused by spirits but not necessarily because of taboo violations. Shamans, mediums, diviners, and sorcerers were all present in Micronesia and consulted by others when manipulation of the spirit world was thought necessary. Formalized cosmologies and hierarchically ranked spirits were more common in those islands that themselves were most stratified.

With this background in mind, the following chapters detail the economic, social, and political life of the peoples from a representative selection of the islands of Micronesia.

Chapter 2
The Western Islands

The three major groups of islands in western Micronesia
are the Marianas, Yap, and Palau. A number of coral
islands--Ngulu, Sonsoral, Pulo Anna, Merir, and Tobi--
are geographically within this area but culturally affiliated with the islands of central Micronesia.

THE CHAMORRO OF THE MARIANA ISLANDS

When Douglas Oliver stated (1951, p. 234) that "the rape
of Oceania began with Guam," he was referring to a predom-
inant theme in Oceanic-European relations, one that has
surfaced time and again since Magellan first burned forty
houses and killed seven men while recovering a stolen
skiff. The people of the Marianas[5] suffered from the
severity of seventeenth-century colonialism not because
there was much of economic value in the Marianas, but
rather because the islands were strategically located on
the Spanish galleon route between Acapulco and Manila,
and because the Spanish world view of the time thought it
essential that pagans be missionized and converted.
    In 1668 a Jesuit mission was established on Guam,
but within two years the Chamorro began to resist forced
conversions and efforts by the missionaries to disband
community clubhouses. Consequently a prolonged period of
warfare between the Chamorro and the Spanish began, a war
which regretfully became one of extermination. Spanish
massacres, introduced diseases, and two devastating typhoons within 30 years reduced an estimated Chamorro population of 50,000 to fewer than 4000 by the early 1700s.
    Although today there are approximately 10,000 native

19

residents in the Marianas (excluding Guam), there are no "pure" Chamorro.[6] The population that has survived is thoroughly mixed with the Spanish, Filipino, American, and Japanese who at various times resided on the islands. Furthermore, there are no communities in the Marianas that are following or possess a "traditional" culture. What we know about traditional Chamorro culture is sketchy and often biased, since it is based on early reports of travelers, missionaries, and government agents. In 1945 Laura Thompson attempted to assemble these data in a reconstruction of precontact Chamorro culture. The summary that follows is primarily based on her work.

The villages of the Marianas ranged in size from 50 to 600 individuals and were found scattered along the coasts of the major islands. Only on the three largest islands--Guam, Tinian, and Saipan--did population density result in the establishment of permanent interior settlements. The Chamorro subsistence economy was based on agriculture, fishing, and a small amount of supplementary hunting (birds, bats, and crabs) and gathering of wild vegetable products. Early reports mention coconuts, yams, breadfruit, several varieties of taro, bananas, and sugarcane as important crops. There is some question about the presence of rice as a cultivated crop in precontact times, but the weight of evidence seems to indicate that the Chamorro did cultivate both wet rice in low-lying swamps and a "dry" variety on higher ground (and thus were the only group in Micronesia to do so).

The agricultural technology was simple and depended on digging sticks and stone-bladed spades. Most agricultural work, from clearing of land and planting through harvesting, was done by men. Women, on the other hand, fished the fringing reefs that surrounded most islands, using small hand nets; occasionally they "stored" part of their catch in fish ponds built of stones along the shore. Women prepared the food for day-to-day consumption by boiling in locally manufactured earthenware pots. For special feasts men cooked large quantities of food in ground ovens excavated for the occasion. Other specialized activities of importance included housebuilding, canoe building, and stone or shell implement manufacture, all the responsibility of men. Plaiting of baskets and mats, pottery manufacture, preparation of medicines, and general domestic chores were done by women.

Chamorro houses traditionally stood several feet above the ground on supporting houseposts. The larger dwellings, men's houses, and clubhouses were supported by stone columns called *latte* (some remains of which can still be seen throughout the Marianas). There are no clear statements regarding the arrangement of houses in a village, although some pictures from relatively late postcontact times show arrangements of houses in orderly rows (Figure 1). This may reflect Spanish regimentation for the purpose of controlling an often hostile population, although Spoehr, in his 1957 archaeological work, noted end-to-end rows of *latte* suggesting a similar aboriginal village pattern. Dwellings within a village were separated according to rank. Sanvitores (quoted by Thompson) said that in Agana on Guam there were "fifty-three principal houses, and of others about one hundred fifty. The latter are low people and are separated from the others who give them no part in the affairs of the town or Court" (Thompson, 1945, p. 12).

Figure 1
Village scene on Saipan, circa 1880. The orderly arrangement of houses may have been forced on the Chamorro by the Spanish. (From Elisée Reclus, *La terre et les hommes*. Paris: Librairie Hachette et Cie.)

Chamorro households were probably made up of an extended family based on a descent line or lineage that was part of a larger matrilineal clan.[7] Within the clan, seniority of descent was emphasized and measured through eldest daughters in the matri-line. Thompson's analysis suggests that decisions were collectively made by the lineage, whose members shared economic rights and obligations.

A slightly more complete picture survives of the complex traditional Chamorro sociopolitical organization. As in all Micronesia, it was based on rank. There were three distinct classes--nobles (*matua*), an elite of high-ranking commoners (*atchoat*), and low-ranking commoners (*mangatchang*). The precise definitions of these classes are not clear, but it is quite likely that rank and class were determined by clan affiliation and land ownership--the nobles and elite were landholders, and the commoners lived and worked on land controlled by one of the other classes. Thompson mentions that the nobles "controlled wealth and exchange" and supplied the highly trained specialists--the navigators, canoe builders, warriors, and fishermen (1945, p. 13). Low-ranking commoners could not become members of the elite, but nobles could lose their position if they were found guilty of a serious offense; their property was confiscated and they were exiled to another district where they were lowered to elite rank.

Thompson suggested that the class system had its origins in multiple migrations to the island; that is, she believed the commoners were descendants of an aboriginal population that was conquered by a superior invading group which formed the elite and noble classes. This kind of theory has been popular in other areas of Micronesia (and the Pacific at large) for explaining class differentiation. Although in some cases interisland warfare, conquest, and colonization (like the Tongan conquest of Samoa and the later Samoan settlements in the southern Gilberts) may explain landed and landless "classes," it becomes difficult to imagine as many multiple migrations and conquests as would be necessary to account for all the class systems of the area. An alternative hypothesis seems in order. In Micronesia social classes are manifestations of a system that emphasizes rank, seniority of descent, and control of land. In those cases where stratification is intense, an ex post

facto explanation for status differences may emerge
based on separate descent, forcefully claimed by members
of high-ranking classes. If such claimants only refer
to descent from different landholding groups, then the
claim is probably accurate, but if they make reference
to separate "racial" origins or separate migrations,
their explanation seems more conjectural.

The major islands of the Marianas were traditionally divided into a number of relatively autonomous districts each under the control of the highest-ranking
chief (*maga* or *maga-lahe*) in the district (who was most
likely the highest-ranking man of the senior clan of the
district). Rank seems clearly related to landholding,
for Thompson noted that district chiefs "controlled
much, if not all, of the district lands and fishing
grounds . . ." (1945, p. 12). Interdistrict warfare and
feuding seem to have been common, and it is probable
that relative status among districts and multidistrict
alliances were in continual flux.

Modern Chamorro life is greatly changed. The
Hispanicization of Chamorro society was certainly the
most important event altering traditional Chamorro culture. Depopulation and forced resettlement by the Spanish of all residents of the northern Marianas on Guam in
the late 1600s were blows from which the traditional
society never recovered, even after the Chamorro were
permitted to return to the northern islands. The Spanish also instituted a policy of appointed *alcaldes* which
contributed to breaking down the authority of the noble
class.

Alexander Spoehr (1954) has itemized some of the
basic changes that have occurred in Chamorro society on
Saipan. The matrilineal clan system has disappeared
completely, at least in part because Spanish, German,
Japanese, and more recently American policies have all
encouraged a patrilineal bias. Family names have been
adopted and are transmitted in the patri-line; land
registration policies have formalized this paternal
identification as well as increased individual ownership
of land. Consequently the solidarity of lineages and
extended families has been destroyed, and today on Saipan the majority of households consist of a nuclear family unit. Where farming is still important, families
may maintain two houses, a village dwelling, which is

the main residence, and a farmhouse located on the family's agricultural land. A man and his sons may thus move between these two residences when working the farm.

Through the 1950s maize was the main agricultural crop in the Marianas and it was cultivated primarily by swidden (slash-and-burn) techniques. At that time a family depending on farmland for subsistence needed approximately three times as much land as was actually under cultivation (at any one time) in order to allow for the fallow cycle common to swidden techniques. There are very few families today, however, that are actually subsistence cultivators; most depend on some form of imported foods and thus they are dependent on wage labor, and possibly marketing of specialized products. This transition has been occurring for some time. As early as 1904 the Germans found it necessary to rule that one-quarter of all farmland must be planted in food crops, since the Chamorro were rapidly converting all land to coconut production in order to obtain a maximum of salable copra. These proceeds were then used to buy imported rice.

Although copra is no longer a source of income for Chamorro on Saipan, the trend toward monetization of the economy has not diminished during the past 70 years. During the years of Japanese administration, sugar was king. Nearly all the land on Saipan was leased to the Japanese and put under sugar cultivation, and the Chamorro subsisted on rents received and plantation wage labor. Since World War II and the beginning of the American administration, the Chamorro have in succession and combination depended on wage labor at military installations and government offices, vegetable gardening for export to markets on Guam, and small entrepreneurial enterprises and craft specializations serving the military and civilian government transients on the island. It may not be accurate to label Chamorro society as either "peasant" in the sense of being tied to a market economy or as consisting of "proletarian" wage laborers, but it does seem accurate to characterize it, after Spoehr, as a "dependent society."

Inheritance of land is now controlled by individuals and nuclear families. Title is assigned to individuals, either males or females, although the majority of land is controlled by the former. A man considers it his duty

before he dies to allot (*partido*) his land to his heirs.
Theoretically both males and females have a right to
equal shares but in fact males usually receive more
since it is thought that a female will be able to depend
on the lands of her husband when she marries. There is
also some reluctance to give land to a daughter, for
there is a possibility that the nuclear family will lose
it when she marries, since she "takes" her land with her
when she marries. Although Spoehr states that a man
does not gain control of his wife's land, he does manage
it and may include it in his *partido*.

J. Jerome Smith (1973) has found a slightly different system of inheritance and tenure on Rota, although it
too derives primarily from Spanish influence. Among the
Chamorro of this island, land is divided so that all eli-
gible heirs receive near equal shares, but "the claim of
a landless spouse is prior to all others, unless the
spouse is no longer actively farming" (Smith, 1973,
p. 12). Two additional rules of some importance are that
a daughter never receives land at the expense of a son,
and that the last married son in a household has ultimate
claim to one house site.

The Chamorro kinship system is now completely bilateral. Other than the nuclear family the only important
kin group appears to be a loose bilateral kindred composed of siblings, parents, siblings of parents, grandparents, siblings of grandparents, their children, their
children's children, and (another Hispanic trait) the
individual's godparents. These are the individuals who
are first approached for aid and who must be informed of
important ceremonial events, like marriages, births,
deaths.

Today the local political system of Saipan and the
rest of the Marianas is patterned on an American model of
municipalities with elected mayors and councilmembers.
The old stratified system of ranked classes of nobles,
elite, and commoners has long since disappeared. Nevertheless in common with the rest of the Micronesians, the
Chamorro still emphasize and respect rank--which is no
longer ascribed by membership in a particular clan or
class but may be achieved through accumulation of wealth.
It seems appropriate to end this description of Chamorro
society, the most acculturated of all Micronesia, on a
note that emphasizes a Micronesian theme of rank and

status, a theme that has been altered in form but which
has survived 250 years of intensive acculturation and
assimilation. In the Marianas *champada* is the desire to
compete for rank and status and, as Spoehr noted in 1954,
it is expressed in many contexts:

> Manuel and his father-in-law, Jesus, started a
> store. At the same time, Jesus' wife's brother,
> Henrici, also started a store next door. Manuel,
> Jesus, and Henrici agreed on a common frontage for
> the two stores. Also, Henrici would sell only
> beer, and Manuel and Jesus only canned groceries.
> After all, they were all relatives and why compete?
> But the first thing Jesus and Manuel knew, Henrici
> was selling canned goods, so Jesus and Manuel
> started selling beer. Then much to Jesus' disgust,
> Henrici built his store out five feet more in
> front. Jesus was angry. So he and Manuel built
> their store out fifteen feet, ten feet beyond
> Henrici's. Henrici bought a small radio, so Jesus
> got a larger one. Jesus' played considerably
> louder, so Henrici hired a man to put up a higher
> antenna. Then his radio played as loud as Jesus'.
> But as soon as this happened, Jesus' daughter ad-
> ministered a real blow by turning the volume up all
> the way on their radio, which had heretofore not
> been so extended. So Henrici bought a new radio,
> which is indubitably larger and louder than Jesus'.
> Henrici went bankrupt, but at least he has the con-
> solation of having the louder radio. Here the
> matter rests. (Spoehr, 1954, p. 305)

THE PALAU ISLANDS

Palau,[8] along with the rest of Micronesia outside the
Marianas, was very little influenced by the Spanish. In
later years when commercial activities in Micronesia increased, first the Germans and then the Japanese took a
more direct interest in the area.

The period of Japanese administration was the era
of Palau's most intensive contacts with the outside
world and hence a period of great acculturation.[9] Angaur
was mined for its phosphates and islanders from through-

out the Mandate were transported to Palau as contract
laborers for the mines. Thousands of Japanese took up
residence in Koror and thousands more visited these islands in the 1920s and 1930s. Many Palauans became
wage laborers either in the towns, mines, or on planta-
tions. Many others gave up their land to the Japanese
through sale, lease, or confiscation. Roland Force
noted in 1960 (p. 73) that "the traditional system of
land inheritance was disturbed so extensively that in
some localities, particularly Koror, it has never entirely recovered." All things considered, however, the Jap-
anization of Palauan culture did not result in as many
radical or permanent alterations of traditional ways as
did the Hispanicization of Chamorro society.

The Palau Islands stretch some 100 miles in a north-
east-to-southwest direction. The largest is Babeldaob
(Babelthuap), which is more than 20 miles long and has a
total area of 153 square miles. The other main islands
of the group are Koror, Peleliu, and Angaur to the south
of Babeldaob, and Kayangel to the north (Map 3). The
12,000 people of Palau reside in villages scattered
along the coasts of the major islands, with a large con-
centration in the administration and commercial center
of Koror. There is some evidence, in the form of abandoned hillside agricultural terraces, that the interior
of Babeldaob was formerly more densely settled. *Colocasia* and *Cyrtosperma* are the staples of Palau but bananas, breadfruit, papaya, sweet potatoes, and manioc
are also important in the diet. Women cultivate the
taro swamps using simple spadelike digging sticks and
knives while the men tend such tree crops as breadfruit,
coconuts, and *Areca* palms (the latter, "betel nut," is
also cultivated and chewed on Yap and in the Marianas).
The men, however, are primarily fishermen who intensively
exploit with spears and nets the coastal waters inside
the fringing reefs.

The nuclear family of the Palauan household is a
segment of a matrilineage, which in turn is part of a
subclan, a clan, and a "clan federation." Postmarital
residence, as Force noted, is usually virilocal: "a
female lived apart from her sib [clan] mates after marriage, ordinarily in a house on land inherited by her
husband from his mother's sib" (1960, p. 46). In this
case matrilineality combined with virilocality results

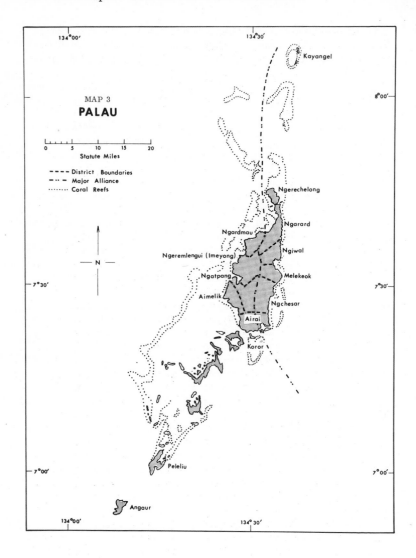

MAP 3
PALAU

Statute Miles

- - - District Boundaries
- · - Major Alliance
········ Coral Reefs

in a degree of flexibility in kin-group membership.
Children can choose, if they wish, to join their father's
matrilineage and thereby gain inheritance rights within
it. Robert McKnight said of this flexibility: "Palauans
emphasize but do not restrict their kinship affiliations
through their maternal line . . . the Palauan will manipulate relationships according to economic and political
advantage" (1960b, p. 42). Because of this ambilaterality a boy may choose to join his father's lineage and
a girl her mother's.[10] Consequently, in Force's words,
"paternal and maternal relations competed for the allegiance of an individual" (1960, p. 48).

Many authors have commented on the competition-
accumulation-manipulation theme that appears to obsess
Palauans. For example, Homer Barnett thought the Palauans' "primary concern is with wealth, and kinship for
them is a vehicle for its manipulation. They use kinship and seek means and excuses to artificially extend
its ramifications because it is only within this frame-
work that they can contrive the wealth displays that
bring prestige and influence" (1949, p. 34). Land is a
basic form of wealth and thus affiliation with the proper
kin group gives one an opportunity to inherit or control
a share of the land of that kin group.

Kin groups, villages, and districts were ranked in
traditional Palauan society, and rank was directly related to wealth both in land and in native valuables.
A certain amount of mobility was possible in the ranking
scheme and this fact encouraged manipulation through
arranged marriages, recruitment of members, and profitable alliances. Clan wealth and clan rank in Force's
words were "positively correlated" (1960, p. 51). One
manifestation of this was seen in an exchange system
which gave control of lineage wealth to the lineage
head--and in this case "wealth" included personnel.
Since a lineage received a bride price from the bride-
groom and his lineage (as well as further compensation
when the woman bore children), a shrewd head arranged
marriages for the women of his lineage to maximize
lineage gain.

Most status and rank competition was kin-group-
oriented rather than individual, but this did not mean
that all lineages and clans were fighting tooth and nail
to raise their status vis-à-vis all others. Competition

was regulated through a dualistic organization--a system
that McKnight termed "controlled conflict" (1960b, p. 18).

Most Palauan clans, although unified in appearance,
were actually divided into two competing "side-legs" or
"other-legs."[11]   Each leg was made up of a number of lineages, and each lineage was composed of a number of closely related households. The actual number of lineages affiliated with one or the other leg varied from clan to clan
and changed through time, as each individual lineage head
made choices that gave his lineage the greatest economic,
social, and political advantage. Manipulation of kin ties
occurred at this level to justify affiliation with one or
the other "more closely related" leg. A lineage that allied itself with a leg of increasing strength might profit
from this decision when the next clan leader was chosen--
who most likely would come from the stronger leg.

Each Palauan village traditionally was settled by
either seven or ten clans which were rank-ordered. The
four highest-ranking clans were thought of as the "original" clans of the village and were called "corner
posts." The eldest man from the highest-ranking lineage
of the highest-ranking clan of the village was the
leader of the village council, where the leaders of all
village clans sat. Seating arrangements for clan representatives in the council house were divided according
to an "other-houses" division. One house alliance, for
example, might include the clans of the first, third,
fifth, seventh, and ninth ranks, while the second alliance was formed of the second, fourth, sixth, eighth,
and tenth ranking clans.[12] In this situation neither
house could dominate the village because neither controlled a decisive majority of higher-ranking members.
Furthermore, the council alliances were usually in a
state of flux. In the preceding example, if house two
could convince the tenth-ranking clan leader to shift
from house one, then house two would dominate the council and the village. This kind of structure no doubt
increased political maneuvering in a Palauan village,
but it permitted even the lowest-ranking group within a
village to hold the balance of power as far as the moi-
ety division was concerned.

Another traditional axis of dualism at the village
level centered on a system of clubhouses. Every village
was physically divided by a path, stream, or some other

feature (perhaps purely symbolic) into two halves. If
the village was large, each half might contain three
men's clubs allied in opposition to the three of the
other half. Smaller villages might have only one or two
clubs in each half. The membership of a club was generally of a similar age grade; one club might have a
majority of old members, another mainly young members.
The old clubs eventually disbanded or retired and were
replaced by new ones. All clubs had members from all
clans of a village. Internally the club was divided into "other-*bai*" that competed in activities or work
(cleaning paths, fishing, thatching) assigned to the
club by the village council. Loyalty to one's club was
a fundamental duty and one might be fined for not par-
ticipating in club activities or for giving aid to a
member of some other club.

Every village also had a women's council and women's clubs or teams that were organized along lines
nearly identical to those of the men. Such organizations could have great influence in running village
affairs, but the women generally lacked the impressive
buildings for their organizations.

Dualism was also an organizing principle above the
village level. Alliances of village clusters were
formed wherein a powerful or large village acted as a
regional capital for a grouping of villages allied to it;
the capital village stood in the middle and the cluster
villages were divided into two halves, each of which lay
to one side of the capital. At one point during their
efflorescence, the four most important capital villages
were Koror, Melekeok, Imeyong (Ngeremlengui), and
Aimelik--then known as the four cornerposts of Palau.

The largest dualistic divisions of Palau were
"other-heavens." The northern and southern (more accurately northeastern and southwestern) heavens embraced a
number of allied districts. The northern group consisted
of Melekeok, Ngiwal, Ngchesar, Ngerechelong, Kayangel,
and half of Airai. The southern heaven was formed by the
alliance of Koror, Ngeremlengui (Imeyong), Aimelik,
Ngatpang, Ngardmau, Peleliu, Angaur, and the remaining
half of Airai. These heavens were traditional enemies
in a continual state of opposition, and in former times
frequent skirmishing and formal battles occurred between
them. Early European traders took advantage of this

opposition and secured their position (at least for a short time) by aiding one heaven in its battles with the other.

Much of this organizational scheme is no longer functioning on Palau, having been replaced by introduced governmental units. Nevertheless, many regional oppositions and alliances in present-day political life can be traced to the traditional groups. Some writers have commented on a class division in Palauan society in which an "elite" or noble class was opposed to a class of "commoners." The elite-commoner distinction was not in actuality a class distinction but rather a classification of seniority of individuals within the clan and village organization. Those individuals of the highest-ranking lineage of the two ranking clans in any village (that is, the leading lineage of each other-house) were elite (*meteet*), while members of all other lineages in the village (including the other lineages of their own clans) were commoners (*chebuuch*).[13] Furthermore, those who were members of the ranking lineages of the two leading clans of a capital village were of higher status than those of the ranking lineages in an outlying village. Thus the highest-ranking elite were the members of the ranking lineages of the four cornerpost villages--Koror, Melekeok, Imeyong, and Aimelik--and as such they were respected throughout Palau.

Palauan social organization was based on rank, determined in part by inherited clan affiliation and in part by personal ability (including manipulation of wealth and kin ties). Traditionally, stability and continuity were possible in this situation because the villages, districts, and the island were split into opposing halves. Individual lineages or clans might change in rank but the village, district, or island continued to be governed as before. Today in Micronesia one often hears Palauans described as power and wealth oriented, full of "get up and go"--certainly praise when voiced by Trust Territory government leaders interested in the development of Micronesia. Similar comments are often made about the Chamorro and their competitive spirit (*champada*). In both cases competitiveness appears to be an expression of a similar underlying principle of organization, one that emphasizes rank.

The Chamorro, in part because of numbers and in

part because of past colonial considerations, have remained localized in the Marianas. Palauans, on the
other hand, have recently been moving from their home islands into administrative and commercial positions
throughout Micronesia. In those areas where rank is
measured along different lines--Yap, for example--com-
petitiveness has led to open anti-Palauan hostility.
One wonders how stable an organizing principle "competition" is without some type of balancing principle, such
as that of the traditional dualistic divisions of
Palauan society.

YAP

The four main islands of Yap[14] lie in a compact group
325 miles northeast of Palau. During German times this
was the administrative center for western Micronesia,
where a cable station was established and where Palauans,
Chamorro, Ponapeans, and Melanesians frequently were
brought as workers by the Germans. In later years when
the Japanese administered the area, a larger community
of colonial officials, traders, and military personnel
grew up around the port of Colonia. In neither of these
cases, however, did the Yapese interact extensively with
the expatriates. Status, success, and achievement in
Yapese society continued to be measured in Yapese terms,
and to the present day Yap has a reputation as one of
the more traditional and "conservative" cultures of
Micronesia.
     Yap is approximately 40 square miles in area and in
1969 had a population of 4380 settled in numerous small
coastal villages. The seasonal rainfall of the area,
soil characteristics, and possibly past agricultural
practices have made the upland interior of the island
unattractive for settlement because of a poor vegetation
cover of savanna grass and scattered pandanus trees.
The dwellings of a village, its meeting area, old men's
clubhouse, and young men's clubhouse are all found close
to the shore. All houses are constructed on elevated
stone platforms and those of the young men's clubhouse
often extend from the beach onto the tidal area of the
reef flat. The young men use the clubhouse as a general
work and recreation area, and those who are unmarried

Figure 2
Gagil, Yap. Most Yapese villages have rocky shorelines
and thus coral-stone jetties are often built onto the
reef flat to facilitate the landing of canoes and boats.

sleep there. Village garden lands are inland on the
grassy slopes which rise behind the coastal foreplain
(Figure 2).

The Yapese subsistence economy is based on fishing
and cultivation of taro (primarily *Cyrtosperma*),
yams (*Dioscorea*), sweet potatoes, and the so-called Tahitian
chestnut (*Inocarpus edulis*). Coconuts, of course, are
important but breadfruit is not frequently eaten. Women
tend the garden crops and do most of the cooking while
men are responsible for fishing and gathering coconuts
and the stimulant *Areca* nuts. The division of labor is
greatly complicated by an extensive system of prohibi-
tions attached to age grades and social classes. Taro,
for example, must be taken from specific appropriate
plots by a woman of comparable age grade status to that
of the person for whom the taro is intended. In all,
there are five age grades--old men, old women, adult men,
adult women, and young women and children. Restrictions
of this type tend to encourage the independence of the
nuclear family in subsistence production. David
Schneider (1949, p. 129) has outlined the system as

follows: "old women cultivate old women's and old men's plots; their young married son and daughter, who form another nuclear family, will take food from plots reserved for young men and other plots reserved for mature women and children. Young women may not even be near plots of old men and old women, and old men take pains to avoid young women's plots." Later in life a widow continues to exploit an old woman's plot for her subsistence as long as possible; a widower, however, may have to depend on taro harvested by his mature son from the old man's plot if he is unable to do it himself and if there is no other appropriate old woman available (Figure 3). The food thus harvested must then be prepared in separate pots over separate fires appropriate to the age and sex grades of the members of the residential unit.

The two important kin groups in Yapese society are the patrilineal lineage (*tabinaw*) and the matrilineal clan (*genung*). Postmarital residence is usually patrilocal; a couple builds a house of their own on a piece of land allotted to them by the eldest member of the patrilineage, who heads the estate and who has nominal control over all estate lands. (This will either be the man's father or his grandfather.) The residential grouping which results is thus built around a man, his sons, and his sons' sons with their in-marrying wives and unmarried daughters. Out-marrying daughters retain some rights in their patrilineage of origin but these are inactive after marriage, since a woman gains rights in the lands of her husband's patrilineage. In case of divorce, however, she has a right to return to her original patrilineage lands.

Genealogically the patrilineage is very shallow. No ties between separate patrilineages are emphasized, and at the death of a patrilineage head fission may occur if the eldest surviving brothers decide to divide the lands rather than keep them in a single parcel with one head. The separate estates that result from such fission may form an association of estates and cooperate in political activities. This is not true in every case, however, since "estates without title and without residual claims to authority lack the motivation to maintain ties with an original estate" (Lingenfelter, 1975, p. 89).

Every plot of land in a Yapese village is named and

Figure 3
Yapese man of Gagil. In the villages of Yap many men
still dress in traditional loincloths and carry various
personal items in a plaited coconut-frond basket.

ranked. The rank of a lineage is derived from the rank of the land it controls and on which it resides. A village is organized around its patrilineages, each of which is represented by its head at village meetings on the *unebai*--an elevated paved area usually found near the old men's clubhouse--where each important lineage head has a reserved seat and stone backrest. A village is divided into two to five ranked wards, each with a chief who is the head of the highest-ranking patrilineage of the ward he represents. The village chief is the head of the most senior patrilineage, which controls the highest-ranking plot of land within the village. Schneider phrased it as follows: "the highest ranking plot of land in each village is the village chief, and the eldest man of the lineage which . . . is held by that land is its spokesman for as long as he is alive" (1962, p. 3). In this sense, as the Yapese saying goes, "the man is not chief, the land is chief."

Schneider makes an interesting point when he says: "the narrow range of the patrilineage helps maintain the elaborate and extreme rank distinctions of both the village and the national political organization by keeping at a minimum the number of persons with equal claims on a particular piece of food-giving or rank-giving land" (1962, p. 4). If lineage depth were greater in Yapese society, one could expect a number of claimants to appear whenever the inheritance of an important piece of land was at hand. By denying lineage depth the Yapese automatically limit the number of heirs and claimants and they also solidify the ranking system. Here lies one basic difference between the Palauan and Yapese systems of rank. The Palauan system is based on a matrilineal clan which usually has great depth and thus results in numerous claimants who potentially can manipulate individual kin ties. In Yapese society these possibilities do not exist, because the patrilineage is shallow and only immediate ties are recognized as legitimate.

The second kin group of importance on Yap is the clan, a dispersed matrilineal, exogamous, named group. All matri-clan members claim descent from its founding ancestress. This group in turn is divided into a number of subclans, each of which includes individuals "who have a known genealogical relationship" (Lingenfelter,

1975, p. 33). The clan functions primarily as a mar-
riage-regulating and mutual-aid group. Clan mates, and
especially subclan mates, are called upon for help in
particular tasks and are obligated to offer hospitality
to a member when he visits villages other than his own.
The clan does not function as a landholding group, although there is usually a particular locality on the island that is associated with the origin of a clan and
may be sacred to it.

Fundamental rank in Yapese society is determined by
caste and class, whereby all villages are inhabited by
members of the same caste and class. Caste is defined
by land ownership--residents of high-caste villages own
the land they inhabit, while residents of low-caste villages reside on land owned by certain patrilineages of
some affiliated high-caste village. The patrilineage
heads of a low-caste village, therefore, only have use
rights to the lands they represent in the village council; nevertheless, their personal attachment to the land
may be as strong as that of a high-caste member. The
relationships between high- and low-caste individuals is
essentially a patron-dependent one phrased in terms of
kinship. A high-caste patron calls his dependent "son,"
and the latter refers to his patron as "father." A low-
caste member may leave the land of his patron anytime he
wishes, and today this type of movement is fairly common.
Such individuals often move to Colonia, the American administrative center of the island.

The system is fixed, however, in the sense that low-
caste people cannot under normal circumstances become
landowners and thus by definition cannot become high-
caste members. Otherwise there are no culturally defined
gross differences between members of the two castes. In
Schneider's words (1949, p. 325), low-caste members "are
neither more nor less intelligent, neither more nor less
inclined to the vices of thievery, greediness, or covet-
ousness, neither blacker nor lighter of skin. Some of
them are intelligent, some not; some are arrogant, some
not; some are good and others bad. The only real difference is that they do not own land."

The high caste is called *pilung* and the low
pimilingai; and each of these is divided into a number
of ranked classes. The high caste has three rank levels
and two different classes in each of the first two

ranks--a total of five classes. The two classes of
chiefly rank are called *ulun* and *bilche*; the two classes
of the second or noble rank are *tetheban* and *metheban*.
The fifth class, that of commoners, is called *dourchig*.
The lower caste is subdivided into four different classes all of different rank--*milingai ni arow*, *milingai*,
yagug, and *milingai ni kan*. These ranked classes form
two main opposing alliances called the "side of the
young men" and the "side of the chiefs," as in Table 2.

The commoner class may decide to ally itself with
either *ulun* or *bilche* chiefs. Residents of the lower-
caste villages, of course, affiliate with the patrons
who own the land they reside on. These alliances are
formed with the object of changing class rank. For example, in a particular district where the side of the
chiefs is ranked higher than the side of the young men,
this rank has been determined by the number of villages
included in the two opposing alliances. In this case
the side of the chiefs has a number of *metheban* and
dourchig noble villages affiliated with it which control important lands of high rank. If the side of the
young men wishes to challenge this ranking, it will have
to build an alliance of obviously greater strength than
that possessed by the side of the chiefs. In doing so,
representatives of the *ulun* village approach its allied
tetheban villages to be sure of their support; then they
approach a number of other *tetheban* villages (perhaps
outside the particular territorial district concerned)
that previously have not been aligned, hoping to gain
their support; and finally they approach unaligned *dourchig* villages (and perhaps some already allied with the
side of the chiefs), promising appropriate rewards if
the villages should join the side of the young men.

Each high-caste village that joins an alliance
brings with it members of low-caste villages resident on
its land. In former times if the side of the young men
felt confident that they had built a stronger alliance,
the leader of this side approached the head of the opposing group and proposed a war to decide the relative
ranking of the two groups. In reality the chief of the
district decided the outcome of the challenge--as he
does today without the war--by informing the two sides
how many warriors each would be permitted to put to battle. On the day of the battle, which might occur either

TABLE 2*

Castes and classes in Yapese society

Caste	Rank	Classes	
		"side of young men"	"side of chiefs"
PILUNG "high caste"	1. chiefly		
	2. nobility	*ulun*	*bilche*
		dourchig	
	3. commoner	*tetheban*	*metheban*
PIMILINGAI "low caste"	1. chief's servants	*milingai ni arow*	
	2. ⎫	*milingai*	
	3. ⎬ serfs	*yagug*	
	4. ⎭	*milingai ni kan*	

*This table is based on information found in Schneider, 1962 and Lingenfelter, 1975. There are some points of difference regarding details of the ranking system.

on land or at sea in canoes, the two sides assembled, skirmished, and withdrew possibly with one or two injuries. The side with obviously superior numbers was declared the victor.

In the preceding case if the challenge of the side of the young men was successful, not only would the two sides be re-ranked, but the successful *tetheban* challengers would now outrank the *metheban* allied with the side of the chiefs, and similarly the *dourchig* villages allied with the side of the young men would be ranked ahead of the *dourchig* who had joined with the side of the chiefs. The rank of the lower-caste villages would similarly be rearranged depending on how their patron villages had fared and also according to how great a service they had rendered their alliance.

Each district on Yap is also an alliance of villages challenging and feuding with other districts. Traditionally there were eight districts (Map 4)[15]; furthermore, these districts were grouped into two opposing super-alliances, centered in the one case on Gagil and in the other on Rull. Tomil, a third center of power, was "balanced between the two alignments, shifting from one to the other as the particular case may require" (Lingenfelter, 1975, p. 127). These two super-alliances were continually maneuvering for superior position in Yap as a whole; and as in the smaller village groupings, rank was altered as one gained or lost active support of villages in comparison with the other alliance. This suggests a second significant difference between the social organization of Yap and of Palau. Not only is the kinship depth lacking in Yap which in Palau permits great personal manipulation to raise rank, but in Yap rank is not raised individually. Changing rank depends on altering the status of an entire class (and hence village) in comparison with some other. There is, then, very little traditional support in Yapese society for individual entrepreneurship.

There are two features of Yapese social organization that promote unity and solidarity rather than opposition and fission. One is the clan, and the other is a scheme of ceremonial exchanges between villages and between segments of villages. Because of the alliances and oppositions in former times, one might be taking his life in his hands if he were to travel beyond the protection of

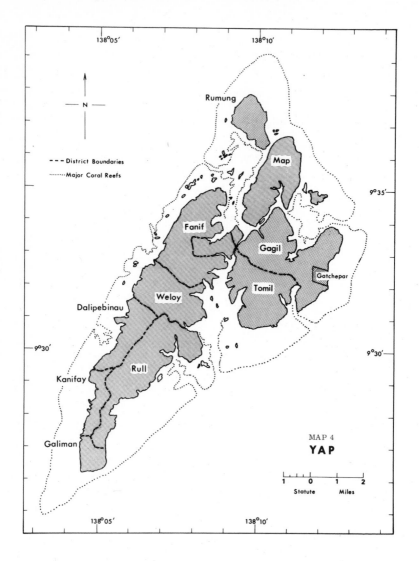

MAP 4
YAP

his own alliance or the security of his own class-
village.   In fact, it is only in recent years that
travel between villages has become common.   Traditionally, if travel were necessary, one invoked common clan
membership as a guarantee of safety, since matrilineal
clans were widely dispersed.   One could thus find a
matrilineal kinsman in even the most distant village who
would be obligated to provide refuge and hospitality.

The second parameter of unity in Yapese society
involves an extensive scheme of ceremonial exchanges
(*mitmit*).   An exchange can be arranged between villages,
wards of villages, or age grades within or between villages.   An invitation is extended from one group to
another and a ceremonial presentation of valuables takes
place.   There are seven different grades of valuables,
the most important being discs made from a particular
seashell and the well-known circular stone "money"
formerly mined on Palau and rafted to Yap.   When an
exchange is arranged with another group, that group is
obligated to return a valuable of equal value within a
year; the exchanges thus established become more or less
continuous through time.

Chapter 3
The Central Islands

The societies of the central Caroline atolls, Truk,
Ponape, and Kusaie constitute the major cultural groups
of central Micronesia. Kapingamarangi and Nukuoro
southwest of Ponape geographically are part of the area
but culturally are Polynesian outliers, having been
settled by back-migrations of Polynesian-speaking peoples.
Ngulu, Sonsoral, Merir, Pulo Anna, and Tobi, on the other
hand, though geographically separated from this region,
were settled by central Carolinian populations.

THE CENTRAL ATOLLS AND TRUK

The atolls and raised coral islands from Ulithi to
Namonuito are settled by peoples closely related to the
population of Truk itself. In all, there are approximately 24,000 residents--5,000 in the central atolls and
19,000 on Truk and nearby islands. The atoll dwellers
of the central Carolines--in contrast to the Yapese, are
well traveled. Most adult males and many females have
visited other islands or atolls perhaps as much as 300 or
400 miles away.

   The islands of the central atolls are all small;
few have as much as 1 square mile of land area.[16] [The
soil is poor and coralline; however, rainfall is abundant, and under normal circumstances the residents are
comfortably self-sufficient, raising enough *Cyrtosperma*
breadfruit, sweet potatoes, and coconuts to support their
small populations.] On those islands with extensive
swampy areas *Cyrtosperma* is usually the most important
crop (Figure 4); where swampland is scarce, breadfruit,

Figure 4
Woleai woman mulching taro field. The large plants are
Cyrtosperma and the small ones, which the woman is
mulching with old banana leaves, are *Colocasia*.

though seasonal, may be equally important when preserved
for off-season consumption. On very small islands such
as Eauripik and Faraulep, where both taro and breadfruit
are more scarce, coconuts are a staple. [Most gardening
activities in the central atolls are undertaken by women;
they cultivate and harvest taro, sweet potatoes, and
with the help of the men, who climb the trees, gather
breadfruit. Men are primarily fishermen, exploiting the
extensive reef areas of the atolls through a variety of
techniques including traps, wiers, nets, spears, hooks,
and lines] (Figures 5 and 6). On those islands that do
not have extensive reef areas, open ocean trolling for

Figure 5
Woleai women reef-fishing. Throughout the Carolines
women reef-fish using hand nets or, as in this picture,
baskets into which minnows are driven with palm-frond
screens.

bonito is also important.

Villages are lineally arranged along the lagoon or
sheltered side of an island. Dwellings may occur singly
or in clusters on a parcel of land that is usually the
seat of a lineage. The important kin groups found in
this setting are the household (descent line), lineage,
subclan, and clan. The central atoll clan (*gailang*) is
a named matrilineal, nonlocalized, and generally exogamous
descent group. Postmarital residence in most of the area
is matrilocal (on Ulithi it is patrilocal), and the
lineage thus formed is the basic landholding and work
group.

Lineages whose members are able to trace a common
relationship are considered members of the same subclan
and this group is the largest kin group with common
inheritance rights. Clan membership gives one a right to
expect hospitality and aid from a clan mate when visiting
another village or island (if one does not have a closer

Figure 6
Woleai men spearing fish caught in a surround net. A
surround net is often set in the lagoon, then pulled
ashore. The trapped fish are either thrown ashore,
speared, or caught with smaller hand nets and transferred
to the accompanying canoes for transport back to the
village.

kinsman), but only in unusual circumstances does common
clan membership alone give one inheritance rights to
land belonging to another subclan.

Several authors have described the society of the
central atolls as unstratified and egalitarian, but this
is only true in comparison to some neighboring, more
stratified society like that of Yap, Palau, or Ponape.
Rank is important in the central atolls, as it is elsewhere in Micronesia, but stratification is less elaborate.
This perhaps is predictable when one considers the
average size of the communities and the meager resource
base of most coral islands. The clans on each island are
ranked--some are chiefly, and others commoner or non-
chiefly. The chiefly status of a clan on one island does
not automatically indicate a like status on any other,
since the Carolinian explanation of chiefly status emphasizes seniority of settlement on the particular island.

Every inhabited island is divided into a number of districts (most commonly either two or three) and each district is represented by a chief who is usually the senior male of the senior lineage of the highest-ranked clan of the district (Alkire, 1965). In some cases there may be a paramount chief who has authority over the whole island; this individual, of course, is drawn from the highest-ranking clan of the island. Even though all clans and chiefs are ranked, it is most common for the chiefs to reach collective decisions in island-wide affairs, often in consultation with the heads of the non-chiefly clans of the island. As often happens in situations such as this, characteristics of personality may be more important in decision-making than actual rank.

A chief has the authority to organize and initiate district or island-wide activities and ceremonies and the responsibility to maintain peace and quiet. It is a chief who decides, for example, when communal fishing expeditions occur, when village paths are cleaned, when a particular ceremony is held, and how long a funeral taboo must last. If someone under his authority breaks the peace or violates a restriction, the chief can impose sanctions on the individual or on the whole population under his jurisdiction. These sanctions most commonly involve some limitation on standard activities, like for-bidding drinking or dancing, restricting fishing in certain areas or perhaps imposing a small fine based on either traditional valuables (such as woven fiber skirts and loincloths) or, more recently, money obtained from the sale of copra. Unlike some other areas of Micronesia, a chief in the central atolls does not have eminent do-main over the land of his district. His authority over land is limited in the same way as that of any lineage head; that is, he is the senior spokesman for the land holdings of the lineage. Nevertheless, a chief has first-fruits rights in his district. At the beginning of the breadfruit season all landholding groups within a district must offer these fruits to the chief, who redistributes them among all the residents of his district or in some cases exchanges them with the chief of another district.

Traditionally there are several levels of supra-island alliance in the central atolls--basically systems of interisland exchange. Three examples are the intra-atoll exchange system (*chülïfeimag*) of Woleai atoll, the interisland "hook" (*hŭ*) centered on Lamotrek, and the overseas system (*sawei*), which involved all of the inhabited islands of the region plus Yap.

The seven inhabited islands at Woleai atoll are so situated that three are found at the western end of the atoll and four at the eastern end. Locally this separation is spoken of as if the islands were located on separate western and eastern lagoons. The reciprocal exchange system links individual districts or islands of the two "lagoons" (Alkire, 1970). For example, Sŭlywäp, an island of the western lagoon, is tied to Ifang district of Falalap island in the eastern lagoon; Tabwogap district of Wottagai island of the western lagoon is tied to Lŭlipelig, another district of Falalap of the eastern lagoon; and so on, so that all the islands in the west are tied to islands in the east. Periodically gifts of coconuts, breadfruit, or fish are made to opposite lagoon partners and jointly the partners control fishing rights over certain reef areas. On important ceremonial occasions, such as the installation of a new chief on one of the islands, the unity of the east in opposition to the west is symbolized through the presentation of a gift of 1000 ripe coconuts to each of the islands of the opposite lagoon attending the installation ceremony. By accepting these coconuts the visitors from the opposite lagoon acknowledge the end of the funeral taboo period for the old chief and the authority of the new chief on his island (Figure 7). The intra-atoll exchange system also permits an island at one end of the atoll to request food from its partner at the other end if the need arises. The system not only serves socially to link the atoll, where an overall paramount chief does not exist, but also it permits a more even distribution of subsistence goods throughout the atoll.

A greater degree of ranking is apparent in the sociopolitical system that links Lamotrek, Elato, and Satawal in an interisland and interatoll exchange system (Alkire, 1965). Lamotrek is the central island of this group and the highest in rank. Through their chiefs the people of Elato and Satawal submit semiannual tribute to the paramount chief of Lamotrek, who in turn redistributes it to the residents of his island. This tribute is in the form of three live sea turtles from Elato and either preserved breadfruit or ripe coconuts from Satawal. The

Figure 7
Men receive gift of coconuts. When a new chief is in-
stalled on one of the Woleai islands, representatives
from the other islands of the atoll attend and receive a
gift of several hundred or thousand coconuts, which are
meant for the residents of the island they represent.

residents of Elato and Satawal gain two rights in return
for their tribute submissions. The first is the right
to exploit various nearby uninhabited coral islands for
coconuts, turtles, and fish which "belong" to the paramount chief of Lamotrek, and second, they have a right
to request food from Lamotrek whenever supplies are
short on their own islands. The "hook" thus is not only
a redistribution system but also an exchange system
based on rank and differential political power.
      The widest exchange system and highest level of
unity in the central atolls is seen in the overseas exchange system (*sawei*), which at its height linked Yap to
all the islands from Ulithi in the west to Namonuito in

the east (Map 1). Until early in this century approximately once a year tribute was delivered to Gatchepar
village of Gagil district on Yap (Map 4) by a fleet of
canoes carrying representatives from nearly all the
outer islands (Lessa, 1950; Alkire, 1965, 1970).

The expedition began in those islands most distant
from Yap, with canoes from Namonuito, Pulap, and
Pulusuk meeting at Puluwat. The representatives from
these islands moved first to Satawal and then to Lamotrek, where a delegate from Elato was also waiting.
When the enlarged fleet arrived at Woleai, representatives from this atoll and from Ifaluk, Eauripik, and
Faraulep joined the expedition. The group left Woleai
and stopped at Fais and at Mogmog island in Ulithi
atoll, and finally arrived at Yap. At each major stop
during the voyage the chief of the highest-ranking
island was in charge of the whole fleet and since, in
general, the rank of the outer islands increased as one
approached Yap, the three most important leaders of the
expedition were, successively, the paramount chief of
Lamotrek, who passed control at Woleai to the chief of
Olimara district of Wottagai island, and finally the
chief of Mogmog, who dealt directly with the Yapese
chief when the expedition arrived at Gatchepar.

The representatives from each of the islands
carried three kinds of gifts called respectively Religious Tribute, Canoe Tribute, and Tribute of the Land.
The first two categories were always in the keeping of
the leader of the expedition; consequently they changed
hands when the canoes reached Lamotrek, Woleai, and
Mogmog. At the end of the voyage the Mogmog chief gave
the Canoe Tribute and Religious Tribute to the chief of
Gatchepar. The representatives of the other islands
passed their Land Tribute directly to the individual
Yapese lineage heads who claimed ownership of the
islands or districts from which the representatives
came. Most of this tribute was in the form of woven
fiber skirts or loincloths, sennit twine, and shell
valuables. The outer-islanders then waited for a seasonal change of winds before setting sail for their
home islands. Before they left, the Yapese usually presented them with countergifts of food and turmeric.

Traditionally the outer islands believed that tribute payments to Yap were necessary; otherwise the

Yapese, because of their superior magic and control of the supernatural, would destroy the outer islands with destructive storms and typhoons. From the Yapese point of view, relations with the outer-islanders were similar to relations with low-caste individuals on Yap itself. The outer-island "children" were permitted to live on and exploit land belonging to their Yapese "fathers," and once a year symbolic recognition of this fact of ownership was manifested in tribute payments. The outer-islanders, of course, viewed the arrangement in a slightly different light, focusing on the environmental realities of the region.

The overseas exchange system (as well as the more restricted intra-atoll and hook systems) linked the people of a number of small, vulnerable, and dispersed islands situated in a typhoon zone of the western Pacific in a way that permitted members of these ranked societies to move freely between islands, and to request and expect aid from any other island within the system in case of disaster and shortages. The system in fact facilitated "everyday" exchange as well, so that normal and/or predictable localized shortages of food, timber, tobacco, and even personnel could easily be balanced. The sociopolitical and kinship ties between the islands made it relatively easy for individuals to move from one island to another if necessary to overcome the uneven distribution of certain classes of individuals (for instance, unmarried men or women). The system was an insurance policy for survival.

Today the outer islands no longer submit tribute to Yap, in large part because the survival value of retaining ties to Yap disappeared several decades ago when the outer-islanders found that foreign colonial governments provided typhoon relief and transport for resettlement of populations. After a destructive typhoon of the early 1900s, for example, the German administration not only provided food relief to the outer islands but also moved populations from the most severely damaged islands to neighboring ones (where in fact some of the survivors still live). The later Japanese and American administrators have had similar policies. Nevertheless, the more localized exchange systems--such as the hook and the intra-atoll system of Woleai--are still important because they operate more regularly, offering immediate aid

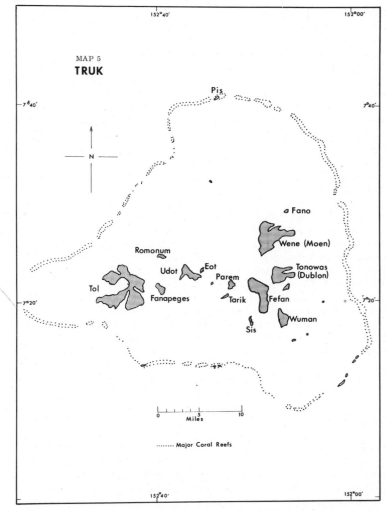

MAP 5
TRUK

Pis

Fano

Wene (Moen)

Romonum

Udot Eot Parem Tonowas (Dublon)

Tol Tarik Fefan

Fanapeges

Wuman

Sis

0   5   10
Miles

········ Major Coral Reefs

during localized shortages that the distant colonial au-
thorities either are unaware of or do not view as crisis
situations.

The Truk islands seem to offer visual proof of Darwin's subsidence theory of atoll formation. The group is
not an atoll but a complex of high islands within a large
lagoon surrounded by an extensive reef (Map 5). Physio-

graphically it has been described as either a complex of coral and volcanic islands or an almost-atoll. The social organization of the inhabitants of the islands might be described in analogous terms as a complex lacking unity or an "almost" unified society.[17]

The land area of Truk is approximately 37 square miles, about the same size as Yap. The 14 main volcanic islands are found scattered within a lagoon 40 miles across. Each of these islands presents a similar appearance: a shoreline of mangrove swamp; a sandy coastal fringe of coconut, breadfruit, pandanus, and hibiscus trees; and an interior of mountain slopes covered with gardens and groves of breadfruit and, at higher elevations, uncut forests. The villages are scattered along the foreshore, but in the not too distant past were often situated in more protected interior locations where they were difficult to attack in the rounds of the nearly constant interdistrict warfare of precontact times. Truk escaped the effects of serious depopulation common in other areas of Micronesia, and at least part of the explanation for this was that the islands were avoided by European sailors, who spread stories of the fierce and belligerent inhabitants (Figure 8).

The social system of the Trukese in its basic structure was very similar to that of the peoples of the central atolls--an understandable similarity since the central Caroline atolls were most likely settled by immigrants moving westward from Truk.

The basic subsistence crop in Truk is breadfruit, a seasonal crop that must be preserved and stored if it is to be relied on during the nonbearing season. Preserved breadfruit is kept in pits dug into the ground and lined with leaves and mats. When needed the pit is opened and a quantity removed and cooked, thus providing a staple with characteristics similar to a strong rich cheese. *Cyrtosperma* and *Colocasia* are grown in lesser quantities.

Gardening and preparation of breadfruit for consumption are responsibilities of men--perhaps two or three working together for several hours two or three days a week (Figure 9). Until recent times the women provided most of the fish consumed, taken from the fringing reefs of the islands. Women did not, however, fish from canoes (a practice forbidden to women throughout Micronesia). Today the women are rarely seen with their small

Figure 8
Trukese man, circa 1880. The distended earlobes with or-
naments and wide shell belt were typically Trukese for
the time. (From Friedrich Ratzel, *The History of Mankind.*
New York: Macmillan.)

Figure 9
Trukese man pounding taro. On Truk men prepare much of
the food for consumption. Here a man pounds taro with
the help of two women while in the background another man
husks coconuts. (Photograph courtesy of Ward Goodenough.)

hand nets working the reefs; most fish are either caught
by the men or taken from cans purchased at local stores
with proceeds from copra sales.

Trukese society is based on a number of matrilineal
clans (*einang*) which regulate marriage. Postmarital
residence is matrilocal, and thus the basic social group
is made up of several sisters and their children, minus
out-marrying males plus in-marrying husbands. This
matrilocal extended family is contained in a group of adjacent dwellings built on lineage land. A man after marriage has labor obligations not only to his wife's
lineage but also to his sisters' (his own) lineage. For
this reason he must spend part of his time visiting the
homestead of his lineage. Usually a man does not marry a
woman from a homestead and lineage too distant from his
own, since this makes the dual call on his services too
difficult to fulfill. If in fact the residence of his

wife is distant from his sister's, the couple may follow
a duolocal residential pattern, spending part of the year
on the wife's land and part of it on the husband's own
lineage land. Several writers have commented on the
brittleness of marriage in Truk and in the surrounding
central Caroline atolls. Marriage, divorce, and remar-
riage seems to be the rule rather than the exception--so
much so, in fact, that the average person (at least before missionization) married three or four times. A partial explanation for this probably lies in the strains
placed on a man because of the dual call on his labor and
divided loyalties between the lineage of his wife and his
own lineage. These divided obligations are most severe
in the case of the senior man of the lineage, for he is
the nominal head of the group and must be consulted on
all major decisions affecting the group. A lineage cannot function efficiently if he resides far from the
lineage homestead.

Under certain conditions patrilocal residence,
patrilineal inheritance, and affiliation with a matrilineage through a patrilineal connection are sanctioned--
a reflection, perhaps, of a bilateral or ambilateral
principle that was much stronger in both Palau and Yap.
These alternative rules for affiliation and inheritance
are invoked in nearly every case where a strictly matrilineal tie is not possible because a lineage has become
extinct. This bilateral bias is such that when a lineage
is nearing extinction, the children of the men of the
lineage have first claim to inheritance even if it is
possible to trace matri-ties to other matrilineages in
the community. The land, in other words, is not reab-
sorbed by the larger subclan or clan through the closest
related lineage, but rather is taken over by the children of the male descendants of the dying matrilineage.
Finally, tradition has it that the clans of Truk were
divided into two moiety-like units, but this dualistic
division has no functional importance today.

Hamlets or villages on Truk are made up of a single
matrilocal extended family or a number of them. Each
lineage is governed by the senior male member of the
lineage and these hamlets are grouped into relatively
autonomous and politically independent districts. Each
island is usually made up of a number of districts.
Aboriginally the larger islands like Tonowas (Dublon)

and Tol each had 18 districts; Wene (Moen) and Fefan had 14 and 11 districts respectively; and the rest of the islands, depending on size, ranged from 10 districts to 1. Although populations may have been somewhat larger in the past, the average district population is around 100, and the average district size seems to be about a quarter of a square mile (Goodenough, 1951, p. 130).

The district chief was traditionally the head of the senior lineage of the district, seniority being measured in terms of priority in settlement, land ownership, and success in battle (which was probably directly related to lineage size). The district chief received first fruits at the beginning of the breadfruit harvest each year, and if one of the lineages or extended families resident in his district did not submit the first fruits, he had the authority to confiscate their lands and reassign them to some other group.

Ranking was probably fundamentally related to control of land. That is, the first lineage to settle an area no doubt made claim to all surrounding lands. Subsequent settlers gained rights either as related kin groups (of lower genealogical rank), or as unrelated groups that moved into the area from elsewhere and received a gift of land, or by moving into the area and obtaining lands through conquest.

Two loose supra-district level confederations or "leagues" were traditionally recognized in Truk. One, called *Sópwunupi* after its ranking clan, was centered on Wene (Moen), and the other, called *Ceún*, was based on Fefan. Wuman was the only major island not affiliated with either league; the districts of this island formed an independent unit. It is noteworthy that "Moen is the island with the largest expanses of taro swamp, and was for this reason the best endowed with food in precolonial times. Districts on other islands in times of food shortage apparently looked to Moen as the source of help and acknowledged Moen's and Sópwunupi's primacy of rank in return--not unlike the situation in the system of relations between Lamotrek, Elato, and Satawal" (Goodenough, personal communication). Fefan, of course, did not make such an acknowledgment, and the numerous wars and diplomatic maneuvers that occurred between these two leagues often depended on the shifting allegiances of districts. "Districts would change from one league to the other in

order to get military help in a feud with immediately
neighboring districts with which they had formerly been
associated" (Goodenough, personal communication). A
major prize obtained in warfare and offered to potential
district allies was fishing rights on the outer reef of
Truk's lagoon. These three power centers--Wene, Fefan,
and Wuman--still wield considerable power in contemporary
Trukese politics.

'   Nevertheless, the dispersed nature of the islands
of Truk made it difficult under aboriginal conditions for
one district and kin group to extend anything approaching
permanent control over an area larger than a single district, and there seem to have been fewer environmental
imperatives to form permanent political unions in Truk
than in the more exposed and typhoon-prone atolls of the
central Carolines. At the time of European contact each
district of Truk was thus primarily an autonomous unit
balanced in a state of precarious peace, engaged in periodic feuding and warfare, and maneuvering in shifting
alliances with surrounding districts. After European
contact administrative policies introduced by the Germans
(and later followed by the Japanese and Americans) grouped
the districts into larger, more permanent political units.

PONAPE AND KUSAIE

The mountainous high island of Ponape lies 380 miles east
of Truk.[18]   It has an area of 129 square miles and sup-
ports 13,000 residents settled for the most part in
scattered homesteads along the coast. The administrative
center of Kolonia is the only significant exception to
this pattern, having attracted large numbers of Ponapeans
as wage laborers.

The staples of Ponapean subsistence agriculture are
breadfruit and yams, but in all more than 40 different
crops are cultivated on this island, where rainfall even
in coastal areas averages more than 180 inches a year. As
in Truk, the more important agricultural crops are tended
by men while women exploit the fringing reefs of the
island with hand nets.

The most common residential group is a small matrilocal extended family that is part of a larger lineage,
subclan, and exogamous matri-clan. Ponape (and tradition-

ally Kusaie) possessed the most complex sociopolitical organization of central Micronesia. The stratification and complexity of ranks and titles on this island stand in sharp contrast to the Trukese system. Why these otherwise closely related islands should be so different is puzzling but may be related to a longer period of settlement and greater population density in pre-contact times on Ponape.

The two territorial divisions on Ponape that are politically important are districts and sections (sub-districts). A section is made up of a number of home-steads and typically runs from the shore to the interior, thus encompassing the full range of land types of the island. The chief of a section is usually the senior man of the senior subclan or lineage in the area. Invariably he is the man who holds the highest title of the section, for the Ponapean political system is built around a series of ranked titles. Since the senior subclan usually controls most of the land within its boundaries, the section chief is in fact steward of its lands. Two lines of titles are found in most sections. In his analysis of Ponapean political organization, Riesenberg (1968) for notational convenience termed these lines X and Y. Within each line are a number of titles, X1, X2, X3 (perhaps up to 10 or 15), and Y1, Y2, Y3, etc., held by the senior men of the section. In some cases every subclan resident in a section holds at least one of the titles while in other cases a single subclan may possess all the titles. The chief of a section--the X1--receives first fruits and tribute from section residents and is responsible for initiating ceremonies, enforcing peace and quiet, and overseeing land use within the section.

Districts are the larger and more important territo-rial units of Ponape. There are five districts (or "tribes," as Riesenberg and some other writers have called them) on the island (Map 6). The political struc-ture of a district is similar to that of a section, with two lines of titles for each district. Paralleling the notation used for section titles, Riesenberg labeled these lines A and B. The two highest titles in each dis-trict are those of *Nahnmwarki* (A1) and *Nahnken* (B1). The sections of a district are divided between these two chiefs; thus some section chiefs in any one district are directly responsible to the Nahnmwarki, while others are

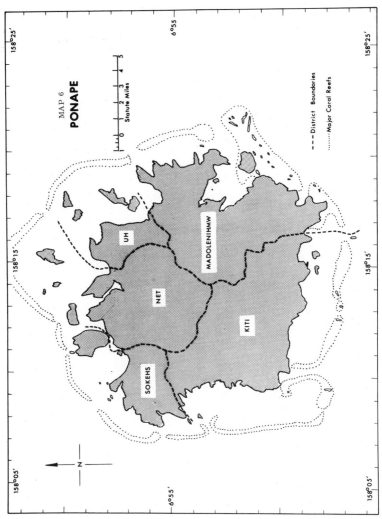

MAP 6
PONAPE

--- District Boundaries
···· Major Coral Reefs

Statute Miles
0 1 2 3 4 5

UH

MADOLENIHMW

NET

KITI

SOKEHS

N

responsible to the Nahnken. Both the A and B lines contain 12 important ranked positions, though in some
districts the total number of titles in each line might
number in the hundreds. District titles traditionally
are monopolized by the two senior clans of the district,
whose rank is determined by order of settlement, subsequent success in warfare, and ultimately control of land.

Furthermore, the more important titles in each line are held by members of senior subclans, determined by descent through eldest sisters of the matrilineage.

One can easily say that in the traditional Ponapean system no two men were of the same rank. The Nahnmwarki and Nahnken were the royalty of Ponapean society, the other title holders the nobility, and the untitled the commoners. (There were female and religious titles as well.) Riesenberg points to the importance that shared title to land had in this order: "Just as the section heads were tenants of the tribal chiefs who owned the sections, or of other chiefs on intermediate levels who in turn held fiefs under higher chiefs, so the commoners were tenants of X1 [section chiefs]" (1968, p. 33).

Although the Nahnmwarki was the ranking title holder in any district and his line of titles "senior," his activities and the activities of the other title holders of the A line were balanced by the power of the Nahnken and the B line. The Nahnmwarki was ill-advised to ignore the power of the Nahnken and his supporters, who in fact might make up a considerable portion of the community (since they controlled half the land in the district). The balanced opposition was symbolized through certain privileged behavior permitted the Nahnken line in the presence of the Nahnmwarki. For example, they could choose to ignore restrictions of manner and standards of behavior and formal speech patterns (which were elaborate in Ponapean society, where different speech forms were required when addressing royalty, nobility, or commoner) required of others in the presence of the high chief. The B line traditionally was viewed as the line of "royal children" and the A line as that of "royal fathers": "at a feast of propitiation . . . if the Nahnmwarki proves too obdurate in forgiving those who are seeking to atone for some offense, the Nahnken might go so far as to violate the sacredness of the Nahnmwarki's head by seizing him and forcing him to drink the proffered cup of kava, which is the sign of forgiveness" (Riesenberg, 1968, p. 50).

In each district, marriage among the ranking subclans supposedly was limited to others of the opposite line; that is, the A line subclan took its wives from B line and vice versa. Since titles were inherited matrilineally, it was possible for a Nahnmwarki to find that

his son (who belonged to the subclan of his mother) was
Nahnken. Similarly a Nahnken might find his son a high-
ranking title holder in the A line--the line from which
the Nahnken had taken his wife. Theoretically one ad-
vanced in rank step by step; when the Nahnmwarki died,
the A2 title holder was promoted to fill the vacancy, and
so on through the top 12 titles of the line. Similarly,
if the Nahnken died, everyone below him in the B line
moved up a step. In reality, however, this did not hap-
pen with any degree of regularity. Someone with a relatively low-ranking title might catapult to the top of a
line if he showed outstanding ability, possessed admired
personal attributes, or proved able at political manipulation (and if those with the final say in promotions saw
some advantage in rapidly advancing him). Decisions regarding promotions were in the hands of the Nahnmwarki
and Nahnken for all ranks below their own in their
respective lines. When the Nahnmwarki himself died, the
Nahnken decided on his replacement and vice versa.

In the ideal pattern one's title (if any) reflected
his genealogical position within the descent group; the
senior man of the subclan held the highest title, the
second most senior man the second title, and so on
through the series. Personal achievement, however, was
and is important in Ponape, and one way of increasing
one's chances of being selected for a top-ranking title
is through prestige competition and feasting. In
Riesenberg's words, "promotions come about in part
through bringing to feasts for presentation to chiefs
larger and better and more frequent food offerings than
other men, thus demonstrating industry, ability, loyalty,
and affection toward the chiefs" (1968, p. 76). Required
first-fruits presentations (which basically are tribute
payments) and voluntary occasional gifts to chiefs are of
equal importance. An ambitious man might find his promotion in the title system measured by his participation
in prestige competitions and first-fruits offerings. The
three most important crops involved in these presentations are yams, breadfruit, and kava (Figure 10).

As in other areas of Micronesia, patrilineal or
ambilateral inheritance choices are made under certain
conditions and thereby one may be affiliated with a descent group other than that of his true matrilineage. If
one ignores the usual matrilineal rules and passes land

Figure 10
Ponape yam.   Men carry a "two-man" yam to a feast.
(Photograph courtesy of Daniel Hughes.)

on to his own children, it is possible for titles to fall
into the hands of previously nonchiefly lineages at the

section level or perhaps be transferred to the opposite line at the district level. Choices such as this were probably more common early in the century during the period of depopulation, when proper heirs were scarce. Some of the anomalies of title holding today no doubt date from this period.

Dualism is built into the Ponapean polity just as it was in another form in Palau. A balanced opposition is maintained between the ultimate authority of the senior line of title holders and the privileged behavior permitted the junior line at both the district and section levels. The extensive list of reciprocal rights and obligations maintained between these two lines led Riesenberg to characterize the system as one of "dynamic symmetry." If intensive European contact with Ponape had been delayed, it is possible that some type of wider supra-district alliances might also have evolved.

Many changes have taken place in the traditional ranking system as a consequence of years of colonial occupation. During the periods of German and Japanese administration, pressure was put on the Ponapeans to accept a patrilineal inheritance system and this resulted in many shifts in title-holding groups. Furthermore, in more recent years new titled positions have been established with the formation of local government councils on an American model. Nevertheless, at those levels of government where performance demands are not completely new, traditional measurements of status still play a significant part in the selection of leaders.

Kusaie, the easternmost high island of Micronesia, possessed a more centralized traditional political system than that of Ponape. The island has a present-day population of 4000 and lies 300 miles southeast of Ponape. It is 42 square miles in area. Kusaie was a major refreshing and replenishing stop for whalers in the 1850s and consequently the culture very early came under unusually intensive acculturative pressures. Protestant missionary work, which began about the same time, led to total conversion by the end of the century. Depopulation also contributed significantly to altering the traditional social organization long before anyone took an analytical interest in its form. Therefore, as in the case of Chamorro culture, one must depend on a variety of historical documents (of varying degrees of reliability)

for a picture of precontact society. In 1968 W. S.
Wilson summarized these data; the following outline is
based on his work.[19]

Kusaie was divided into four districts and each of
these was composed of a number of subdistricts (totaling
57 for the island). Districts and subdistricts extended
inland from the coast, but most communities were found
along the shore while garden areas were inland. Men
cultivated breadfruit and taro with the simple technolog-
ical inventory common to Micronesia, and women fished
the fringing reef. Although the data are not entirely
clear, it appears that residential and landholding groups
were based on matri-clans, subclans, and lineages.

Lelu district, centered on a small island just off
the coast of Kusaie proper, was the highest-ranking district and the seat of the paramount chief (*tokosa*). This
chief resided in a guarded capital city surrounded by a
hierarchy of retainers. If this picture is accurate,
then Kusaie was the most centralized of all Micronesian
chiefdoms. In fact, the power of the Kusaien paramount
chief seems to have been known as far away as Truk, where
legendary histories rank him above all other chiefs in
the Carolines.

Including the paramount chief there were 18 chiefly
titles on the island, divided into two subclasses--nine
high titles and nine low. The paramount chief, who of
course was at the top of the high-title line, had the
authority to grant other titles and allocate lands to be
administered by each title holder. In turn the low-
ranking title holders had a voice in selecting the paramount chief when that office fell vacant.

The vast majority of Kusaiens, of course, were not
title holders but commoners (*metsisik*) who lived on and
worked lands under the authority of a particular chief.
These individuals gave a percentage of their produce as
tribute to their district chief, who in turn passed half
of it on to the paramount chief in Lelu. Wilson noted
that three levels of rights to land, "the common title,
chief's title and king's title (seizure)" (p. 28), tied
the political system closely to basic land tenure. Furthermore, it is quite likely, as in other areas of
Micronesia, that actual membership in a kin group was
closely associated with (if not defined by) rights to
particular parcels of land. Genealogical manipulations,

land transfers, and prestige feasts were involved in winning promotion in the scheme of titles.

Primarily as a consequence of missionary influence the importance of titles began to decrease in the middle and late nineteenth century. By 1960 only two title holders survived and their titles had lost political significance. Nevertheless, rank is still important to a Kusaien, but prestige is now measured either through control of church affairs or, more recently, through positions established in the American administration of the island (which is part of the Ponape District, Trust Territory of the Pacific Islands). The church and the American municipal system have offered mobility to many who would have had fixed status in the old system.

Although the hierarchical, highly centralized system of old no longer functions, Kusaien society at the village level is still dependent on subsistence cultivation of breadfruit, taro, and bananas. Postmarital residence is usually patrilocal unless an alternative choice offers a couple greater potential gain. Membership in descent groups is still defined by rights to particular land parcels. Residents of a village are organized into a number of subgroups, usually three, which cooperate and compete with one another in village tasks. Two leaders are chosen from each village and these leaders meet to select two all-Kusaien leaders. There are female groups in each village, which organizationally mirror the men's groups. The interplay of activities between the three village groups, two village leaders, and two all-Kusaien leaders is certainly reminiscent of the more traditional Micronesian ideals of balance in political organization.

Chapter 4
The Eastern Islands

The Marshalls and the Gilberts are the two archipelagoes
of eastern Micronesia, an area that also includes the
more isolated individual raised coral islands of Banaba
(Ocean Island) and Nauru. The Marshalls are part of the
Trust Territory of the Pacific Islands, the Gilberts and
Banaba (which is no longer inhabited) are a colony of
the United Kingdom, and Nauru is an independent republic.

MARSHALL ISLANDS

The 29 atolls and 5 raised coral islands of the Marshalls[20] have a total land area of only 74 square miles
and a total population of some 20,000. If the population
were evenly distributed throughout the chain--which by no
means is the case--this would result in a population
density of approximately 270 per square mile. To the
outside world the Marshalls are probably the best known
islands of Micronesia largely because of the atomic bomb
and missile testing that has taken place there. Most
people have heard of Bikini, Eniwetok, and Kwajalein,
but far fewer have ever heard of Majuro, Jaluit, and
Ailinglapalap, three of the more important inhabited
atolls.
    The archipelago is divided into two parallel chains,
Ratak to the east and Ralik to the west (Map 1). The
atoll islands of the Marshalls are similar to those of
the central Carolines but are often considerably longer,
stretching along the reef for 10 or perhaps 20 miles. In
addition, rainfall in the northern islands is more limited, a condition that restricts agricultural production.

Few of these islands have large enough quantities of
breadfruit or taro for these crops to play a significant
role in the diet. Traditionally the northern Marshallese
depended on coconuts, pandanus, and arrowroot as dietary
staples.

The basic land division of the Marshalls, called a
wato, is a strip which runs from the lagoon to the ocean
side of an island. One or more of these strips are held
and administered by a matrilineage or descent line. The
men of the residence plant crops, harvest, and fish along
the reef and in the lagoon. The primary crop in the
northern areas was pandanus, and traditionally late in
the year men spent a large part of their time gathering,
preparing, and preserving this fruit--a process which required scraping, steaming, pounding, mixing with arrowroot, and drying. In the southern atolls, on the other
hand, breadfruit production was important--so important
that during harvest season most other activities were
postponed while the crop was prepared for preservation.
The women of a household were responsible for day-to-day
cooking, either in ground ovens or over open fires.
Today most communities have become dependent on a cash
economy derived from copra sales and consequently rely on
purchased imported foods.

Marshallese society is composed of a number of
matrilineal clans (*jowi*) which are nonlocalized, exogamous descent groups similar in form to those described
in the central Carolines. The most important corporate
descent group is the lineage (*bwij*), which is first and
foremost a landholding group with a seat at a particular
wato. The lineage head (*alab*), usually the eldest male
of the senior line of the lineage, is steward of the
lineage land holdings. Ordinary lineage members work the
lands and pass a percentage of their produce to the
lineage head, some of which he keeps and some of which he
passes on to those higher-ranking political figures who
have rights in the land involved. A residential group
can range in size from a nuclear family to a large
extended family of 20 to 25 members. In the case of
large and important parcels of land there is a tendency
to avunculocal residence, the result of men clustering
around the lineage head either with the hope of reward or
in anticipation of succession. In some cases patrilocal
residence may be followed if it should prove economically

profitable. Nevertheless, except for lineage heads who
live on the lands they control (and therefore with their
own lineages), most ordinary men live with their wives'
lineages, perhaps returning periodically to contribute
labor to their own lineage.

Leonard Mason (1954), who studied Bikini in the
northern Marshalls, reports that lineage solidarity and
the matrilocal/matrilineal rules were more often followed
on that island than Spoehr (1949) found was the case on
Majuro in the southern Marshalls (Map 7). Spoehr noted
a distinct bilateral tendency in Majuro society, and
Kiste (personal communication), who has studied the resettled Bikini population on Kili (Kiste, 1968), feels
that bilaterality is just as important there as in Majuro. In both these cases the residential group was a
bilateral extended family. Often each nuclear family
had its own sleeping house, but all such houses were
clustered around a central cookhouse where food was prepared for all residents.

All writers agree that control of land is a basic
theme of Marshallese culture. Title is divided and
shared by several levels of the society. The common members of a lineage have use rights, and although in traditional times a chief theoretically could dispossess
them since he held ultimate title, he would have been
foolish to do so, for his wealth depended on their labor
and tribute payments. In effect, a chief's power cor-
responded to the number of commoners in his realm. Sym-
bolizing these levels of ownership were two basic levels
of titles. The lowest and most important in day-to-day
affairs was the lineage *alab*, who organized and directed
lineage activities and allotted lands for use to different descent lines within the lineage. The second level
was that of the chiefs (*iroij*) who held title over an
island or atoll. A third kind of title was that of
bwirak, individuals on the "fringe of nobility"--to use
Mason's terminology--who, being descended from mixed
commoner/chiefly marriages, did not have full chiefly
rights.

Shortly before initial European contact a chief of
Ailinglapalap was able to extend his control over most
of Ralik (except Eniwetok and Ujelang). Periodically
thereafter the occupant of this office made a circuit of
these islands with his retainers to collect tribute. The

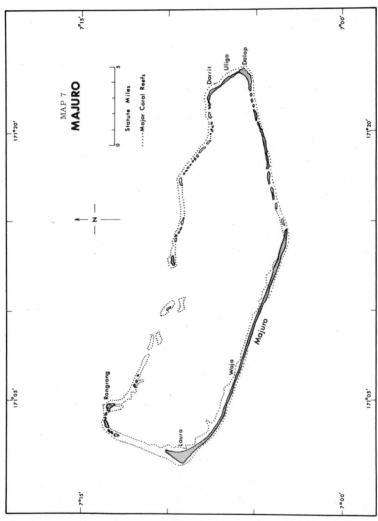

MAP 7
MAJURO

Statute Miles

····· Major Coral Reefs

Darrit
Uliga
Dalap

Rongrong

Laura

Woja

Majuro

chain subsequently was divided into two districts, one
including Namu and the islands north, the other Jabwot,
Ailinglapalap, and the islands south. Although all of
these islands were "owned" by the paramount chief, he
rarely called at those further north than Kwajalein and
Ujae, largely because they were somewhat isolated and
too impoverished to provide any worthwhile tribute.

Within the northern islands themselves, stratification was less elaborate in comparison to those of the south.

Ratak was similarly organized but far less central-ized. The whole chain was never unified under a single paramount chief, although the chief of Maloelap was able to put the islands to the north (except for Mejit) under his control. Majuro and Arno broke away from this alli-ance, however, and again became independent political units. The Ralik and Maloelap alliances thus were both in a state of flux and varied in size as local chiefs tested the strength of their islands vis-à-vis the para-mount chief. This tendency toward fission encouraged the paramount chief to move his residence from island to island to make his control clearly visible to the local district chiefs.

Interisland travel in the Marshalls was almost as important as in the central Carolines. The sailing canoe of the Marshalls was a finely worked craft probably supe-rior in design and efficiency to the Carolinian craft. Although the threat of typhoons is largely absent in the Marshalls, travel was stimulated for economic, social, and political reasons. Interisland marriage was common, as was adoption, and both encouraged movement between islands in order to visit relatives or exploit land re-sources. The political organization just outlined also encouraged travel for collection or delivery of tribute, exploitation, and warfare.

Whereas central Carolinian navigation was based on a highly refined star compass and celestial observations (Alkire, 1970; Gladwin, 1970), Marshallese techniques emphasize the interpretation and analysis of currents and wave patterns. The Caroline chain lies in an east-west line and therefore the apparent east-west movement of the stars over the islands can be utilized to advan-tage by emphasizing points of rising and setting stars. In the Marshalls, on the other hand, most traditional voyaging was generally north and south, since travel was usually limited to islands within the same chain, either Ralik or Ratak. The Marshalls reach farther north than do the Carolines, and consequently many of the islands experience a longer and more reliable trade wind season. The archipelago lies at right angles to these prevailing winds and the easterly sea swell carried before the winds. Since the atolls and reefs are generally quite long and closely spaced, they interrupt the smooth transit of the swell; therefore, the basis of Marshallese navigation focused on interpreting the patterns, orientation, intensity, and direction of deflected waves. The easterly swell is deflected in a predictable and constant pattern as it passes through the islands; the trained navigator, therefore, is able to judge his position when out of sight of land by reading surrounding wave patterns, conceptually tracing the origins of the particular pattern back to a known reef or island of the chain.

The famous Marshallese stick charts are mnemonic aids used in teaching various wave patterns to apprentice navigators (Davenport, 1960). A stick chart is made from a number of interconnected thin strips of wood ordered and affixed to each other to represent the pattern of waves between and around several islands and reefs (represented on the chart by small shells or coral pebbles tied to the strips). The navigator identified the islands of the chart, then set a course from one to the other, observing the pattern of curved and intersecting strips representing waves and currents he would encounter on the particular voyage.

Today life in the Marshalls, as in the rest of Micronesia, is an amalgam of the new and the old (Figures 11 and 12). Nearly half of the Marshallese population has moved from the more distant atolls and islands either to the administrative center at Majuro or to Kwajalein atoll where they are employed at the United States missile testing grounds. The presence of this latter station has seen the Marshallese population of Ebeye, a small islet where Marshallese workers live, grow from 500 people in 1950 to over 4000 in 1970. Ebeye is a community entirely dependent on wage labor and imported foodstuffs. Forced population movements have also occurred in the Marshalls. A Bikini chief is said to have announced the decision of the residents of his atoll following a request by the United States, in words obviously dated by the events of the 25 years that have since passed:

> . . . if the United States government and the scientists of the world want to use our island and atoll for further development, which with God's blessing will result in kindness and benefit to all mankind, my people will be pleased to go elsewhere. (Mason, 1954, p. 2)

This group has since been given permission to return before long to Bikini from Kili where they were resettled.

Figure 11

Arno men perform traditional stick dance. This type of
dance is still seen in the outer islands of the Marshalls.
Under missionary influence the Marshallese long ago
adopted western clothes but occasionally assume traditional decoration for special ceremonies. A similar kind
of stick dance is also performed throughout the Caroline
islands. (Photograph courtesy of Jack A. Tobin.)

The residents of Eniwetok were similarly removed to
Ujelang and have not yet obtained permission to return
to their home atoll.

Nevertheless in other areas of the Marshalls--dis-
tant from port towns and military installations--life
has continued with less change. The political power of
paramount chiefs has been altered by the imposed structures of German, Japanese, and currently American admin-
istrations, but the general hierarchical ranking of the
society remains. The importance of the *alab* in lineage
affairs and the division of rights to land among individuals and lineages also persists. Spoehr (1949a, p. 78)
saw the importance of the land tenure system in this con-
text when he noted a "close relation of the class structure to the system of land tenure." Other writers have
viewed the system in the same way. Mason (1954, p. 171)
stated: "Attitudes about land constituted one of the
most important motivations underlying Bikinian social,

Figure 12
Village scene on Arno Atoll (1950). Many Marshallese
houses are now roofed with corrugated iron. (Photograph
courtesy of Jack A. Tobin.)

economic, and political life." And Tobin (1958, p. 3),
who has written extensively on Marshallese land tenure,
continually emphasizes how this domain is basic to
Marshallese culture, dominating Marshallese thought:
"People are always plotting to obtain more land. Today
this takes the form of marriage negotiations. In the
past not only marriage was used but also the means of
warfare and black magic."
    Now with the decreasing number of sanctions which
a paramount chief can impose, settlements are reached
and alliances made through more subtle political and
economic manipulations.
    Robert Kiste (1974, p. 4) more recently has observed:

    . . . the competition over land represents more than
    a preoccupation with a particular resource; rather,
    it is but one manifestation of a larger set of re-
    lated interests. Marshallese attitudes and be-
    haviors reveal a generalized concern over the dis-
    tribution and acquisition of power, influence,

privilege, and control, not only of land but of
all resources which they deem of substantial worth.

Political schisms, indeed, may now be more common.
Both Spoehr (1949a) and Tobin (1953) have described in
detail one such case of fission on Majuro atoll. Majuro
is divided into four districts all of which in the past
were under the authority of a single paramount chief.
Early in the last century, however, a "civil war" broke
out over succession at the death of the reigning paramount chief. In later years a cleavage in the royal lineage resulted when two cousins both claimed the office.
In traditional times similar disputes undoubtedly occurred and were probably settled by mustering lineage supporters, both noble and commoner. Warfare may have forced
settlements in a certain number of these cases. Fission-
ing of lineage descent lines is after all a common process
in segmentary lineage and clan systems such as this. In
the Majuro case, however, because of legal limitations
imposed by the Germans (and later the Japanese and
Americans), no decisive move was possible by either branch
of the lineage. Instead an uneasy balance was reached in
which the island was divided between the two claimants
and their descent-line followers. Subsequent years have
seen numerous political moves, countermoves, manipulations, and machinations by both lines as attempts are
made to gain dominance over the opposing line. Most
such moves involve land transactions.

Similar divisions were found on many other atolls
of the area. For example, territorial divisions were at
one or another time also present on Arno and on Eniwetok.
And in the latter case, when the population was moved to
Ujelang it was agreed that this newly inhabited island
should similarly be divided between the two chiefly
lineages.

In summary, the Marshallese sociopolitical system
traditionally was a ranked one. Stratification possibly
decreased somewhat in intensity as one moved north into
the poorer and more marginally productive islands.
Although Marshallese ideology emphasized matrilineality,
as often as not bilateral choices were made. In several
areas a balance was maintained between opposing political
districts or islands, and at the height of the traditional period these were often combined into petty states
ruled by a paramount chief who periodically collected
tribute from outlying islands. At that time warfare

(and more recently political and economic manipulation
of land holdings) periodically shifted boundaries and
altered alliances.

THE GILBERT ISLANDS AND NAURU

The Gilbert Islands form the eastern and southernmost
extension of Micronesia.[21]   Some 35,000 people are settled
on the 11 atolls and 5 raised coral islands of the group.
The southern islands of the chain are among the more
marginally productive areas of Micronesia, in large part
because of erratic and unpredictable rainfall, which on
Tabiteuea, for example, averages 32 inches per year.
Rainfall increases as one moves north in the chain, from
61 inches per year at Tarawa to 137 inches at Makin and
Butaritari. And apparently stratification in traditional
society increased as productivity (and rainfall) increased,
since the northern Gilberts were the most stratified and
centralized and the southern Gilberts the least.
   In the northern Gilberts breadfruit is the staple
crop, supplemented by *Cyrtosperma*, coconuts, and pandanus.
Farther south, however, where droughts are common, breadfruit is of minimal importance, and pandanus and coconuts
are the staples, to the extent that Grimble (1933-1934)
labeled the Gilbertese "a pandanus people." Whereas
breadfruit is preserved in the northern islands, in the
south only pandanus flour and coconut toddy taffy are
stored. Toddy is obtained from the coconut palm by tap-
ping the bound inflorescence of the tree two or three
times a day and collecting the sap in a coconut-shell
container. The sweet sap is rich in vitamin B and no
doubt is highly significant in contributing to a balanced
diet among the Gilbertese. If the sap is allowed to fer-
ment for eight to ten hours, a palm wine is obtained that
is consumed by men. The sweet toddy, on the other hand,
may be boiled down to the consistency of a sticky taffy
candy, which is stored for short periods and is important
as a food during periods of drought.
   Men plant and harvest coconuts, pandanus, and breadfruit. They also fish the lagoons, distant reefs, and
open ocean, and care for artificial fish ponds found in
the interior of most islands. Milkfish (*Chanos chanos*)
are farmed in these areas. Their fry are gathered from
the reef and transferred to the ponds where the grown
fish are later harvested. Women cultivate (often helped

by the men) the *Cyrtosperma* gardens, prepare pandanus flour and coconut toddy taffy for storage, and are responsible for the preparation and cooking of daily meals.

In precontact times Gilbertese settlements were scattered in hamlets along the lagoon shore of an island. Clusters of dwellings generally housed a corporate descent group on its own land--a strip similar to the Marshallese *wato* extended from lagoon to ocean. Not long after colonial rule was established, however, the British for administrative convenience forced the populations of individual islands and districts to concentrate in nucleated villages in single-family dwellings. This residential change had far-reaching effects on the structure of Gilbertese descent groups. Unlike most of the rest of Micronesia, the people of the Gilbert islands did not emphasize matrilineal descent in the formation of corporate groups. In this respect there is some variation between the northern and southern islands that warrants discussing them separately.

In the northern Gilberts ambilineality is the principle of organization. An individual can actively participate in any kin group he is able to trace a relationship to through any ancestor. The actual descent group that results from this rule is the "ramage" (*utu*), an ambilineal group in which all members trace descent through a combination of males and females to a founding ancestor. All members of this group share inheritance rights to ramage lands. Such ambilineal links permit one to claim descent and membership in more than one ramage depending on the male or female link chosen in each ascending generation and the number of generations one chooses to trace back. In the northern Gilberts in recent times an individual commonly does not remember ancestral links more than two or three generations distant, but even this gives one potential residential and exploitation rights in five or six different household clusters.[22] In actual fact, at marriage a couple usually takes up residence at a site where the parents or grandparents of either husband or wife previously resided. The final choice reflects the greatest advantage in land or status that the couple has. This wide range of choices means that there is little chance that unilineality will emerge as a consistent pattern even though there is a preference for virilocal residence. When a residential choice is made, one becomes a member of a residential "core" ramage called the *kainga*, a word which also denotes the main house site or seat of the ambilineage. This group naturally is of greater importance to the individual than the other ramages he potentially belongs to through other ambilineal links.

Each ramage has a head, and the ramage heads meet in council at the district meeting house (*maneaba*) to discuss matters affecting the whole district (Figure 13). Decisions are made at this time concerning feasting and competitions, and construction and repair of district public structures such as meeting houses and district fish ponds. Stratification in northern Gilbertese society is similar in complexity to that of the southern Marshallese. Traditionally each island had a paramount chief who in most cases claimed eminent domain over the island and who, in fact, represented the ramage that controlled the largest number of land parcels. Although this chief resided in a particular district, he received food presentations from the other districts. The leaders of the other districts were descended from "aristocrats" who had been given land rights in the form of authority to expect and collect tribute from residents and holders of particular land parcels by an island chief; the aristocrats, therefore, were kinsmen of the chief and individuals descended from earlier island chiefs. The island chief divided these rights among his kinsmen (probably his brothers), and they as district chiefs received tribute and passed some of it on to their higher-ranking brother. Finally, district chiefs allotted land within their domain to commoner residential ramages.

Even though Makin and Butaritari were ruled by a single paramount chief, and in precolonial but post-contact Gilbertese society the chief of Abemama was able to extend his control beyond his own atoll (to include Kuria and Aranuka atolls), interisland travel was extremely limited in comparison with either the Marshalls or the central Carolines. Warfare was limited for the most part to interdistrict disputes reflecting power plays between brothers or aristocrats descended from brothers. Nevertheless, these disputes seem to have been frequent and severe enough to have resulted in elaborate offensive and defensive paraphernalia. The Gilbertese were known among all Micronesians for their sharks'-teeth spears and daggers, and for their protective armor of woven coconut sennit coir (Figure 14).

In the southern Gilberts there were no island-level paramount chiefs, and thus the meeting house was and is of greater importance in organizing district affairs.

Figure 13
A meeting house on Tarawa Atoll.   An example of the traditional *maneaba* of the Gilberts.   (Photograph courtesy
of Richard Shutler, Jr.)

Ramage heads traditionally had fixed sitting places in
the district meeting house based on the rank of the ramage in the district.   New seats might be created as a
result of ramage fission; and ramage fission occurred
through fragmentation of land holdings.   Postmarital
residence in the southern islands was more commonly virilocal, and therefore a patrilocal descent group tended
to develop.   Furthermore, residential kin groups in the
past appear to have been larger and more stable, thus
giving the ambilineal ramages the outward appearance of
patrilineal descent groups even though structurally they
were based on the same rules as those in northern Gilbertese society.
     Nauru is a single raised coral island historically
isolated by location, prevailing currents, and minimal
seafaring on the part of its inhabitants.[23]   Linguistically
Nauruan is only distantly related to Gilbertese, and
Nauruan society in some ways seems more similar to
"nuclear Micronesia" (Marshalls and Carolines) than to
the Gilberts.   This island and Banaba (Ocean Island),
which conversely is closely related to the Gilberts,
are rich in phosphates that have long been mined by

Figure 14
Gilbertese warrior, circa 1880. This warrior wore a full
suit of armor woven from coconut sennit twine and carried
a shark's-teeth spear. (From Friedrich Ratzel, *The
History of Mankind.* New York: Macmillan.)

European interests. Unlike Banaba, however, the island has not been abandoned by its native population; rather the Nauruans are attempting to use their share of the proceeds of the phosphate mining to build an independent and viable system that will survive when the mines themselves have been exhausted. At this time the Nauruans have the highest per capita income in the Pacific (and perhaps the world).

The island is 12 miles in circumference and has a permanent population of 4000. Traditionally the residents depended on a subsistence economy based on the staples of coconuts, pandanus, and coconut toddy. Coconuts and toddy were gathered by men who also fished offshore waters. Both men and women participated in the seasonal pandanus harvest and women gathered shellfish from the onshore fringing reef. The interior brackish lagoons or lakes (of which Buada lagoon is the largest) were used for raising milkfish in a way nearly identical to that described for the Gilberts (Figure 15).

Nauruan dwellings were constructed to accommodate an extended family and were found clustered in hamlets along the coastal belt of the island. The island was divided into 14 districts and only one of these was cut off from the coast but centered on Buada Lagoon (Map 8). Matrilineal clans controlled marriage but seem to have had minimal importance in control of land. Wedgwood (1936, p. 374) felt that "in no sense were . . . homesteads clan property; they were individually owned and might even pass into the possession of a member of another clan--for in Nauru both men and women own land and give it . . . to both sons and daughters and even unrelated friends." Nevertheless, there was a tendency toward matrilocal marriage, and therefore a woman, her sisters, and their daughters formed a descent-line residential unit within which most property was probably transmitted. Inheritance through one's father did occur, and Wedgwood cites this as one fact that tended to weaken matrilineal allegiance and even shift alliances at the district level.

There were three status classes in Nauruan society. Members of the senior rank (*temonibe*) were those individuals descended from the eldest daughter of a clan foundress. Those descended from a younger daughter consequently were of junior rank (*amenengame*). The third class was a small group of "serfs," individuals who had fled their home villages during warfare and subsequently placed themselves under the protection of a higher-status

Figure 15
Buada Lagoon on Nauru. Milkfish are farmed in ponds on
Nauru and throughout the Gilberts.

landholder in another hamlet or district.
     Membership in senior or junior rank had implications
for land ownership, since most land was passed on in the
senior line of a clan. Kinship linkages must have been
juggled from time to time with the intention of gaining
inheritance rights. Ernest Stephen (1936) noted that
most disputes in Nauru concerned land--a familiar theme
for the whole of Micronesia.
     Lineage heads imposed taboos and organized district
activities such as singing and dancing competitions, kite
flying, and capture of frigate birds. On Nauru (and in
the Gilberts) frigate birds were caught and, when possible,
tamed. High-ranking men owned a number of these birds
kept tied to racks erected near the shore where they
acted as decoys for wild birds (Figure 16). The latter
were caught with weighted bola-like slings when they
flew nearby.
     The 14 districts of Nauru probably developed as
separate political units after contact with Gilbertese
and Europeans. At the very least, Wedgwood believes

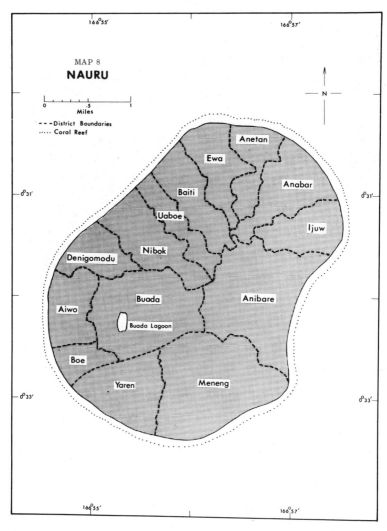

MAP 8
NAURU

0   .5   1
Miles

−−−District Boundaries
····· Coral Reef

Anetan

Ewa

Anabar

Baiti

Uaboe

Ijuw

Denigomodu

Nibok

Buada

Anibare

Aiwo

Buada Lagoon

Boe

Yaren

Meneng

the district chief to be a postcontact innovation. Increasing interhamlet and interdistrict warfare inten-
sified stratification and eventually resulted in supra-
district centralization. Two opposing alliances emerged.
The first included the districts of Ijuw, Anabar, Anetan,
Ewa, Baiti, Uaboe, and Nibok; the second Anibare, Meneng,
Yaren, Boe, and Aiwo. Denigomodu and Buada, the two

Figure 16
Nauru men and tame frigate birds, circa 1930. Bird racks
were erected along the shore, and the tame birds tied to
them acted as decoys for wild frigate birds. (From
Albert F. Ellis, *Ocean Island and Nauru*. Sydney: Angus
and Robertson.)

remaining districts, vacillated in their affiliation
depending on the nature of the dispute and the persua-
siveness of relatives in one or the other alliance. If
these districts decided to align themselves in a dispute,
the decision was made by the heads of the ranking lineages (the main landholders). The "swing" power that
these two districts possessed also permitted them to act
as mediating forces.

Chapter 5
Conclusions
The Traditional Adaptation

The ten Micronesian societies that have been described
display differences in details of material culture, techniques of subsistence exploitation, and form of sociopolitical organization, but of greater importance are
the underlying similarities of these cultures. Common
heritage, common adaptation, and diffusion have all
played a part in shaping the regularities.

Some of the most obvious similarities, especially
in material items (tools, utensils, canoe types, design
motifs, etc.), undoubtedly spread through diffusion. In
both the central Carolines and Marshall Islands purposeful long-distance voyaging served to maximize the proba-
bility that a trait or idea developed on one island
would soon be carried to many others. In the past, even
the most isolated island outside the range of purposeful voyaging experienced the arrival of drift canoes
from time to time. Survivors of one of these voyages
undoubtedly spread a number of traits from one island
and area of Micronesia to another. Beyond this, however,
there are a number of underlying similarities in sociopolitical organization that cannot be explained solely
on the basis of diffusion, for they involve trait complexes which conceivably one group would adopt only in
preference to already established patterns under prolonged pressure, revolution, or some other unusual circumstances. These regularities more likely have their
basis in a common proto-Micronesian (Austronesian)
heritage.

Certainly ranking and stratification are universal
parameters of Micronesian culture. This fact has sur-
prised a number of analysts, since many of the coral

islands of the region have small populations and are
marginally productive. In these cases, of course, emphasis on rank is usually less intense than on the high
islands, since any organizational principle is shaped
by the adaptive necessities of particular environmental
settings. Nevertheless, it is universally present and
in those intensely stratified societies--Palau, Yap,
Ponape, and Kusaie--rank is expressed through, and consequently controlled by, some form of dualistic balance.

A further generalization that can be made about
Micronesian sociopolitical institutions--including the
kinship system--is that they are founded on the control
of land. In 1948 George P. Murdock suggested that
Micronesian kinship systems evolved from a bilateral
form. By way of evidence he cited the presence of a
Hawaiian type of generational kinship terminology and
the limited development of unilineal terminology (name-
ly, modified forms of Crow terminology in the central
Carolines and Iroquois terminology in the Marshalls)
even in areas with strong matrilineal kin groups. He
proposed that the matrilineal systems developed when a
consistent rule of residence (in most cases matrilocal)
began to be followed. Evidence which has accumulated
since Murdock's analysis--some of it from other areas of
the Pacific--tends to support the assumption of a bilateral basis for proto-Micronesian culture. Furthermore,
it appears more and more likely that unilineal kin groups
developed because of a close identification of a residential kin group with particular land parcels and inheritance rights to such parcels. Not only does the evidence from the strongly matrilineal areas of Micronesia
support this conclusion, but also that from Yap (with a
double descent system) and the Gilberts (ambilineal
groups) emphasizes, in different contexts, the close
identification of Micronesian kin groups with particular
land holdings and residential choice.

Western geographers attached a name to Micronesia
that serves to emphasize the area's outstanding environmental characteristic--near-microscopic islands scattered across some two million square miles of ocean. The
view that Micronesians take of their environment recognizes this same reality, but whereas we tend to focus
on the vast expanse of ocean, they invariably emphasize
their homes, the minute pieces of land. The generally
high population density common to the area, especially
in precontact times, meant that nearly all potentially

productive land in Micronesia was either directly or
indirectly exploited for subsistence purposes (and more
recently commercial ones). The scarcity of such productive land in most areas naturally increased its value
and consequently man's adaptation to this limited resource not only shaped the subsistence economic systems
but other social, political, and religious institutions
as well. In Micronesia one can not only say that land
is life in the sense that land provides the basic sus-
tenance for survival, but also that land is a way of
life, since throughout Micronesia the basic social institutions have been molded by adaptation to the concept and
reality of limited land.

In pre-European contact times, the Micronesian
islands were isolated from the epidemic diseases that
effectively controlled and reduced populations in other
regions of the world. Consequently, on many of these
islands, natural population growth eventually placed
strains on available resources. The near universality
of land disputes in the societies described are witness
not only to present conditions but also, in many cases,
to these former conditions. In earlier times warfare,
feuding, and interisland systems of trade and exchange
also served to alleviate problems associated with high
population density and the resulting temporary or
long-term shortages of resources.

Severe depopulation occurred on many of the islands
after contact with European and other metropolitan powers
in the late eighteenth and early nineteenth centuries.
The Micronesians had little or no immunity to the many
diseases introduced at this time; in addition, they were
easy victims to slave raids and forced migrations. As
population densities fell, competition for land also
became less severe and warfare less necessary (or less
feasible as pacification was enforced by a succession of
colonial governments). Similarly, those systems of
interisland cooperation and exchange that had developed
often diminished in importance as populations declined
and as colonial administrators reorganized local political systems.

By the 1930s the Micronesians were widely viewed as
one more example of a "dying race." Fortunately this
dismal prediction never came to pass and, ironically,
the advances in medical care and changes in political
organization that grew out of World War II led to a
reversal in Micronesian population trends.

Today all Micronesian populations are increasing at an annual rate of between one and three percent. The near future will bring a reemergence of those population problems that confronted the precontact ancestors of present-day Micronesian peoples. Warfare is no longer an option for solving such problems, and it would seem that some form of interisland cooperation is once again necessary. Either this or the Micronesians will probably become completely dependent on outside forces for their survival. Many of these problems, associated with Micronesian metropolitan power interaction, are discussed in the following chapter.

Chapter 6
Modern Developments

The cultural changes in Micronesia precipitated by contact with metropolitan powers have varied from island to
island.[24] From the mid-1800s Europeans have actively
engaged in the copra trade, initiated plantation cultivation of other crops, and exploited various marine resources (whales, trepang, fish). These commercial enterprises led to increasingly frequent contacts with
Micronesians that inevitably brought about many social
and cultural changes. Some of these have been discussed
in earlier chapters.

   Several of the larger islands of Micronesia--Palau,
Yap, Ponape, and Jaluit and somewhat later, Majuro--be-
came centers of colonial administration and commercial
activity. The port towns that grew up at these centers
stimulated further change. Migration from outlying
areas and islands increased, economic exchanges were
rapidly monetized, and, in furtherance of colonial or
missionary policies, formal schools were established. As
a consequence these communities began to develop in con-
formity to metropolitan social and political models.
Those members of the local community who received Western
training soon formed a new elite, often challenging the
authority of the old. Older extensive kinship loyalties
were weakened as wage labor favored the nuclear family
and patri-ties took precedence (in the eyes of several
colonial regimes) over matri-ties.

   For a number of reasons, foremost of which were
isolation and relative economic poverty, few of these
changes reached into the outlying areas until the military events leading to and including World War II.

In Micronesia this war above all accelerated political
change. World War II signalled a change in colonial
political authority, but more important, it marked here,
as in most other areas of the world, the beginning of
the end for colonialism. For much of Micronesia, however,
the same strategic locale that once marked the islands
for early colonization also contributed to a late decolonization. Presently it is within the area of political development that change is most rapidly taking place
in most of Micronesia.

Nauru is one of the few islands of Micronesia that
has had a continuing economic importance since the early
1900s for a succession of colonial governments, and
ironically it was the first island of Micronesia to be
decolonized. The rich phosphate deposits of the island
have been exploited by the Germans, Japanese, British,
and Australians. Following World War II, Nauru was
designated a United Nations Trust Territory, a political
status similar to that given the Carolines, Marianas, and
Marshalls, the Trust Territory of the Pacific Islands
(TTPI). Nauru, however, was administered by the
Australians and the TTPI by the Americans. The latter
territory also had the distinction of being designated
a "strategic trust," thus singling the TTPI out for
special consideration of the Security Council of the
United Nations. The status of Nauru, in contrast, could
be altered by the General Assembly without fear (or
protection) of a Security Council veto. Consequently,
the economic viability of Nauru, in combination with
shrewd Nauruan negotiations and General Assembly pressures, brought political independence to the island on
January 31, 1968.

Independence is a status that is soon expected for
the Gilbert Islands as well. Great Britain appears eager
to move in this direction even though the economic viability of the Colony is far less secure than that of
Nauru. Once their independence is granted, this will
leave the TTPI as the only remaining non-self-governing
colonial area of Micronesia.

The future status of the TTPI is currently under
negotiation and the problems that confront the nego-
tiators are in many ways typical of many "micro-states"
of the Pacific. As such they warrant detailed discus-
sion here.

The TTPI is divided into six administrative units,
designated the Marianas, Yap, Palau, Truk, Ponape, and

Marshalls districts. The first significant step toward an all-districts or "national" level of self-government occurred in 1965 when the United States Secretary of the Interior authorized the establishment of the Congress of Micronesia. This congress is a bicameral elected legislature, but initially it had little more than an advisory function to the executive offices of the High Commissioner, an officer appointed by the United States Secretary of the Interior.

Nevertheless, the congress provided a forum where representatives (who were by and large members of the Western educated new elite) of all districts could exchange ideas and exert pressure, when deemed necessary, on the administration. In 1969, as the result of both internal and external pressures, the first round of talks between representatives of the United States government and a committee of the Congress of Micronesia was scheduled to negotiate a mutually acceptable future political status for the TTPI.

The Micronesian delegation entered the discussions with four negotiating principles: (1) that sovereignty in Micronesia resides in the people of Micronesia and their duly constituted government; (2) that the people of Micronesia possess the right to self-determination and may therefore choose independence or self-government in free association with any nation or organization of nations; (3) that the people of Micronesia have the right to adopt their own constitution and to amend, change, or revoke any constitution or governmental plan at any time; and (4) that free association should be in the form of a revocable compact, terminable unilaterally by either party.

The "free association" status proposed by the Micronesians was one modeled after that negotiated between New Zealand and the Cook Islands. The Micronesians were seeking full control over internal affairs while giving the United States government authority in external affairs and defense.

The United States delegation's counter offer was one of "commonwealth status" similar to the current United States-Puerto Rican arrangement. This was rejected by a majority of the Micronesian delegation, but thought acceptable (and desirable) by the Marianas representatives. The negotiating unity of the Micronesian delegation began to crumble.

The real deadlock in negotiations (as far as majority
opinions were concerned) lay in the fourth principle of
the Micronesians, and this principle was not accepted by
the Americans until 1972 at the fifth round of negotiations; and it is thought that this occurred only because
the Marianas meanwhile had undertaken separate negotiations with the United States for commonwealth status.
For the Congress of Micronesia delegation, the fifth
round produced a "partial draft compact of free association," covering areas of internal affairs, foreign
affairs, and defense. Articles of the compact that remained to be negotiated included financial assistance,
trade and commerce, immigration, and travel.

The wording of the draft and the three years that
had passed since the opening of negotiations produced
some second thoughts among other members of the Congress
of Micronesia, however. When the document was presented
to the full congress it was strongly criticized for giving a balance of power to the Americans. The congress
believed that Micronesian authority over internal affairs
would be compromised by such phraseology as that found
in Title II:

> The government of the United States shall have full
> responsibility for and authority over all matters
> which relate to the foreign affairs of Micronesia,
> *notwithstanding any other provision of this compact*.
> (Joint Committee on Future Status, 1972) [Emphasis
> mine.]

Consequently, the full congress instructed the
political status delegation to open discussions on independence as an alternative for Micronesia at the next
round of talks with the Americans, *and*, at the same time,
complete details on the remaining articles of free association. At this next meeting, however, the United States
delegation refused to proceed unless a clear objective
were in sight--either free association or independence.
The fragile unity of the congress, which had begun to
crumble when the Marianas undertook separate negotiations
with the United States, was now strained even further.

Two plebicites were held in Micronesia in the summer
of 1975. The first occurred in the Marianas where the
voters of that district elected by a 78% majority to
accept commonwealth status. The second was held in the
rest of the districts of the TTPI and was meant to

provide some lead to the Congress of Micronesia on the course it should pursue in its future negotiations with the Americans. Unfortunately, in this case the results were less decisive; some districts favored independence, others free association, and yet others a continuance of the current status of Trust Territory.

The Congress of Micronesia had meanwhile continued along the lines suggested by the political status delegation and authorized the calling of a constitutional convention. The constitutional convention convened on Saipan, still the seat of Micronesian government, in July 1975 shortly after the results of the two plebicites were made public (Figures 17 and 18).

The constitutional convention delegates decided to proceed as though they were developing a document for an independent nation, the rationale being if free association were the eventual status agreed upon, it would be easier to alter the draft constitution along these lines than vice versa. In the course of the constitutional convention proceedings, the long-standing problems revolving around traditional versus modern cultural forms, economic viability, and national unity quickly surfaced.

Delegates to the convention included both traditional chiefs and elected representatives. The traditional chiefs from several districts were cautious in their approach and suspicious that the constitution might usurp or undermine their local authority. For several of these individuals, in fact, the calling of the convention marked a point where they began to take seriously the implications of political change. Until this time they had tended to view the Congress of Micronesia as either a mediating body that acted as a buffer between themselves and the American administration, or as a harmless and sometimes amusing debating society. The implications of the constitutional convention were that the Congress of Micronesia, or some similar body, would become a real power. Consequently, several proposals were put forward in the convention with the intent of protecting traditional chiefly authority. One such proposal, made by the chiefly delegate of Kita district, Ponape, was that a "chamber of chiefs" be authorized in the constitution that would have "advisory" power on all Micronesian government measures, and veto power on "matters affecting tradition" (*Pacific Daily News*, August 22, 1975). Under this proposal, the chamber of chiefs would not introduce legislation but would review all bills coming from the other house or houses of the legislature.

Figure 17

Figure 18

The bulk of the other delegates to the convention represented Western educated elite who often opposed the traditional chiefs, but who did not form a unified block on all matters. The two main factions within this group were made up, on the one hand, of Congress of Micronesia members who were also elected to the convention and, on the other hand, young members of the civil service and

other Micronesian employees of the TTPI government. The
Congress of Micronesia block generally wished to push
ahead with a draft constitution entailing aspects of
independence or free association. The civil servant/ TTPI
employee block generally was more cautious and interested
in practical problems of finance and governmental transition.

The most serious problems initially facing the convention, and threatening unity, concerned the allocation
of power between the current districts and any proposed
national government. The delegates from the more populous
districts favored a bicameral legislative structure with
representation based on population; those from the smaller
districts supported a unicameral legislature with equal
representation for all districts. Those delegates from
"rich" districts preferred a national government of limited power, while those from the poorer districts maneu-
vered for some sort of guarantee that all tax monies
would be equally distributed.

Various aspects of these problems led to an initial
boycott of the convention by the Marshallese chiefs and
threats of withdrawal by the Palauans. In the end, the
unity of the convention was maintained through compromise
and the draft constitution that emerged on November 8,
1975 clearly reflected this (Appendix I). The main
points of the document included (1) a unicameral congress (Article IX, sect. 8) that compromises between
representation on the basis of state equality and population numbers (Article IX, sect. 20); (2) a system of
tax redistribution (Article IX, sect. 5) that guarantees
that half of the revenues collected in any state will be
returned to that state by the central government; and
(3) protection of the status of traditional chiefs
(Article V, sect. 1). A resolution (number 32) was
passed by the convention and appended to the constitution
that attempted to clarify this last point. Sections 1
and 4 of Article X in the constitution also stipulate
that the chief executive (President) of the federation
will be elected by the congress from among its own
members.

The draft constitution was accepted by the delegates
without dissent, although after returning to their home
districts several denied wholehearted support.

The potential for further complications and compromises in political development arose within the next
six months when the Congress of Micronesia Joint Committee on Future Status resumed negotiations with the

United States government. On June 2, 1976 a statement
on the agreements reached at these meetings was released
(Appendix II). Several of these understandings could
conflict with clauses in the draft constitution, especially in the areas of foreign affairs and citizenship
versus "nationals" rights.

The reality of strategic location has certainly
influenced all these discussions on the future course
of decolonization just as it had influenced some 400
years of colonial status. "Rich" districts were rich
because of locale--the Marshalls because Kwajalein had
been selected as a United States missile testing site; the
Marianas because of their proximity to Guam (and United
States military installations) and Japan; and, potentially, Palau, as it recently has been approached by
Japanese, United States, and Iranian interests who hope
to establish a deep-water supertanker port at the north
end of Babelthuap Island.

Even if interdistrict political differences should
continue to be resolved through compromise, the future
of any unified Micronesia will be confronted by hard
economic facts and the periodic resurfacing of interdistrict rivalries and competition based on language
differences, traditional status and culture, and that
ever present variable of "strategic locale."

Appendix I

Draft Constitution of the
Federated States of Micronesia

PREAMBLE

WE, THE PEOPLE OF MICRONESIA, exercising our inherent
sovereignty, do hereby establish this Constitution of
the Federated States of Micronesia.

With this Constitution, we affirm our common wish
to live together in peace and harmony, to preserve the
heritage of the past, and to protect the promise of the
future.

To make one nation of many islands, we respect the
diversity of our cultures. Our differences enrich us.
The seas bring us together, they do not separate us.
Our islands sustain us, our island nation enlarges us
and makes us stronger.

Our ancestors, who made their homes on these islands,
displaced no other people. We, who remain, wish no
other home than this. Having known war, we hope for
peace. Having been divided, we wish unity. Having been
ruled, we seek freedom.

Micronesia began in the days when man explored seas
in rafts and canoes. The Micronesian nation is born in
an age when men voyage among stars; our world itself is
an island. We extend to all nations what we seek from
each: peace, friendship, cooperation, and love in our
common humanity. With this Constitution we, who have
been the wards of other nations, become the proud guard-
ian of our own islands, now and forever.

ARTICLE I: TERRITORY OF MICRONESIA

Section 1. The territory of the Federated States of
Micronesia is comprised of the Districts of the Micronesian
archipelago that ratify this Constitution. Unless limited by international treaty obligations assumed by the
Federated States of Micronesia, or by its own act, the
waters connecting the islands of the archipelago are
internal waters regardless of dimensions, and jurisdiction
extends to a marine space of 200 miles measured outward
from appropriate baselines, the seabed, subsoil, water
column, insular or continental shelves, airspace over
land and water, and any other territory or waters belonging to Micronesia by historic right, custom, or legal title.
Section 2. Each state is comprised of the islands
of each District as defined by laws in effect immediately prior to the effective date of this Constitution. A
marine boundary between adjacent states is determined by
law, applying the principle of equidistance. State
boundaries may be changed by Congress with the consent of
the state legislatures involved.
Section 3. Territory may be added to the Federated
States of Micronesia upon approval of Congress, and by
vote of the inhabitants of the area, if any, and by vote
of the people of the Federated States of Micronesia. If
the territory is to become part of an existing state,
approval of the state legislature is required.
Section 4. New states may be formed and admitted
by law, subject to the same rights, duties, and obligations
as provided for in this Constitution.

ARTICLE II: SUPREMACY

Section 1. This Constitution is the expression of the
sovereignty of the people and is the supreme law of the
Federated States of Micronesia. An act of the Government in conflict with this Constitution is invalid to
the extent of conflict.

ARTICLE III: CITIZENSHIP

Section 1. A person who is a citizen of the Trust Territory of the Pacific Islands immediately prior to the

effective date of this Constitution and a domiciliary of a District ratifying this Constitution is a citizen and national of the Federated States of Micronesia.

Section 2. A person born of parents one or both of whom are citizens of the Federated States of Micronesia is a citizen and national of the Federated States by birth.

Section 3. A citizen of the Federated States of Micronesia who is recognized as a citizen of another nation shall, within 3 years of his 18th birthday, or within 3 years of the effective date of this Constitution, whichever is later, register his intent to remain a citizen of the Federated States and renounce his citizenship of another nation. If he fails to comply with this Section, he becomes a national of the Federated States of Micronesia.

Section 4. A citizen of the Trust Territory of the Pacific Islands who becomes a national of the United States of America under the terms of the Covenant to Establish a Commonwealth of the Northern Mariana Islands may become a citizen and national of the Federated States of Micronesia by applying to a court of competent jurisdiction in the Federated States within 6 months of the date he became a Unites States national.

Section 5. A domiciliary of a District not ratifying this Constitution who was a citizen of the Trust Territory of the Pacific Islands immediately prior to the effective date of this Constitution, may become a citizen and national of the Federated States of Micronesia by applying to a court of competent jurisdiction in the Federated States within 6 months after the effective date of this Constitution or within 6 months after his 18th birthday, whichever is later.

Section 6. This Article may be applied retroactively.

ARTICLE IV: DECLARATION OF RIGHTS

Section 1. No law may deny or impair freedom of expression, peaceable assembly, association, or petition.

Section 2. No law may be passed respecting an establishment of religion or impairing the free exercise of religion, except that assistance may be provided to parochial schools for nonreligious purposes.

Section 3. A person may not be deprived of life, liberty, or property without due process of law, or be denied the equal protection of the laws.

Section 4. Equal protection of the laws may not be denied or impaired on account of sex, race, ancestry, national origin, language, or social status.

Section 5. The right of the people to be secure in their persons, houses, papers, and other possessions against unreasonable search, seizure, or invasion of privacy may not be violated. A warrant may not issue except on probable cause, supported by affidavit particularly describing the place to be searched and the persons or things to be seized.

Section 6. The defendant in a criminal case has a right to a speedy public trial, to be informed of the nature of the accusation, to have counsel for his defense, to be confronted with the witnesses against him, and to compel attendance of witnesses in his behalf.

Section 7. A person may not be compelled to give evidence that may be used against him in a criminal case, or be twice put in jeopardy for the same offense.

Section 8. Excessive bail may not be required, excessive fines imposed, or cruel and unusual punishments inflicted. The writ of habeas corpus may not be suspended unless required for public safety in cases of rebellion or invasion.

Section 9. Capital punishment is prohibited.

Section 10. Slavery and involuntary servitude are prohibited except to punish crime.

Section 11. A bill of attainder or ex post facto law may not be passed.

Section 12. A citizen of the Federated States of Micronesia may travel and migrate within the Federated States.

Section 13. Imprisonment for debt is prohibited.

ARTICLE V: TRADITIONAL RIGHTS

Section 1. Nothing in this Constitution takes away a role or function of a traditional leader as recognized by custom and tradition, or prevents a traditional leader from being recognized, honored, and given formal or functional roles at any level of government as may be prescribed by this Constitution or by statute.

Section 2. The traditions of the people of the Federated States of Micronesia may be protected by statute. If challenged as violative of Article IV, protection of Micronesian tradition shall be considered a compelling social purpose warranting such governmental action.

    <u>Section 3</u>.   The Congress may establish, when needed, a Chamber of Chiefs consisting of traditional leaders from each state having such leaders, and of elected representatives from states having no traditional leaders. The constitution of a state having traditional leaders may provide for an active, functional role for them.

ARTICLE VI: SUFFRAGE

<u>Section 1</u>.   A citizen 18 years of age may vote in national elections.   The Congress shall prescribe a minimum period of local residence and provide for voter registration, disqualification for conviction of crime, and disqualification for mental incompetence or insanity.   Voting shall be secret.

ARTICLE VII: LEVELS OF GOVERNMENT

<u>Section 1</u>.   The three levels of government in the Federated States of Micronesia are national, state, and local. A state is not required to establish a new local government where none exists on the effective date of this Constitution.

    <u>Section 2</u>.   A state shall have a democratic constitution.

ARTICLE VIII: POWERS OF GOVERNMENT

<u>Section 1</u>.   A power expressly delegated to the national government, or a power of such an indisputably national character as to be beyond the power of a state to control, is a national power.

    <u>Section 2</u>.   A power not expressly delegated to the national government or prohibited to the states is a state power.

    <u>Section 3</u>.   State and local governments are prohibited from imposing taxes which restrict interstate commerce.

ARTICLE IX: LEGISLATIVE

<u>Section 1</u>.   The legislative power of the national government is vested in the Congress of the Federated States of Micronesia.

<u>Section 2</u>.   The following powers are expressly delegated to Congress:

   (a)   to provide for the national defense;

   (b)   to ratify treaties;

   (c)   to regulate immigration, emigration, naturalization, and citizenship;

   (d)   to impose taxes, duties, and tariffs based on imports;

   (e)   to impose taxes on income;

   (f)   to issue and regulate currency;

   (g)   to regulate banking, foreign and interstate commerce, insurance, the issuance and use of commercial paper and securities, bankruptcy and insolvency, and patents and copyrights;

   (h)   to regulate navigation and shipping except within lagoons, lakes, and rivers;

   (i)   to establish usury limits on major loans;

   (j)   to provide for a national postal system;

   (k)   to acquire and govern new territory;

   (l)   to govern the area set aside as the national capital;

   (m)   to regulate the ownership, exploration, and exploitation of natural resources within the marine space of the Federated States of Micronesia beyond 12 miles from island baselines;

   (n)   to establish and regulate a national public service system;

   (o)   to impeach and remove the President, Vice-President, and justices of the Supreme Court;

   (p)   to define major crimes and prescribe
           penalties, having due regard for local
           custom and tradition; and

   (q)   to override a Presidential veto by not
           less than an 3/4 vote of all the state
           delegations, each delegation casting one
           vote.

Section 3.   The following powers may be exercised concurrently by Congress and the states:

   (a)   to appropriate public funds;

   (b)   to borrow money on the public credit;

   (c)   to promote education and health; and

   (d)   to establish systems of social security
           and public welfare.

Section 4.   A treaty is ratified by vote of 2/3 of the members of Congress, except that a treaty delegating major powers of government of the Federated States of Micronesia to another government shall also require majority approval by the legislatures of 2/3 of the states.

Section 5.   National taxes shall be imposed uniformly.   Not less than 50% of the revenues shall be paid into the treasury of the state where collected.

Section 6.   Net revenue derived from ocean floor mineral resources exploited under Section 2 (m) shall be divided equally between the national government and the appropriate state government.

Section 7.   The President, Vice-President, or a justice of the Supreme Court may be removed from office by a 2/3 vote of the members of Congress.   When the President or Vice-President is removed, the Supreme Court shall review the decision.   When a justice of the Supreme Court is removed, the decision shall be reviewed by a special tribunal composed of one state court judge from each state appointed by the state chief executive. The special tribunal shall meet at the call of the President.

Section 8.   The Congress consists of one member elected at large from each state on the basis of state equality, and additional members elected from congressional districts in each state apportioned by population. Members elected on the basis of state equality serve for a 4-year term, and all other members for 2 years.   Each member has one vote, except on the final reading of bills. Congressional elections are held biennially as provided by statute.

Section 9. A person is ineligible to be a member of Congress unless he is at least 30 years of age on the day of election and has been a citizen of the Federated States of Micronesia for at least 15 years, and a resident of the state from which he is elected for at least 5 years. A person convicted of a felony by a state or national government court is ineligible to be a member of Congress. The Congress may modify this provision or prescribe additional qualifications; knowledge of the English language may not be a qualification.

Section 10. At least every 10 years Congress shall reapportion itself. A state is entitled to at least one member of Congress on the basis of population in addition to the member elected at large. A state shall apportion itself by law into single member congressional districts. Each district shall be approximately equal in population after giving due regard to language, cultural, and geographic differences.

Section 11. A state may provide that one of its seats is set aside for a traditional leader who shall be chosen as provided by statute for a 2-year term, in lieu of one representative elected on the basis of population. The number of congressional districts shall be reduced and reapportioned accordingly.

Section 12. A vacancy in Congress is filled for the unexpired term. In the absence of provision by law, an unexpired term is filled by special election, except that an unexpired term of less than one year is filled by appointment by the state chief executive.

Section 13. A member of Congress may not hold another public office or employment. During the term for which he is elected and 3 years thereafter, a member may not be elected or appointed to a public office or employment created by national statute during his term. A member may not engage in any activity which conflicts with the proper discharge of his duties. The Congress may prescribe further restrictions.

Section 14. The Congress may prescribe an annual salary and allowances for members. An increase of salary may not apply to the Congress enacting it.

Section 15. A member of Congress is privileged from arrest during his attendance at Congress and while going to and from sessions, except for treason, felony, or breach of the peace. A member answers only to Congress for his statements in Congress.

Section 16. The Congress shall meet in regular, public session as prescribed by statute. A special session may be convened at the call of the President of the Federated States of Micronesia, or by the presiding officer on the written request of 2/3 of the members.

Section 17.

    (a)   The Congress shall be the sole judge of the elections and qualifications of its members, may discipline a member, and, by 2/3 vote, may suspend or expel a member.

    (b)   The Congress may determine its own rules of procedure and choose a presiding officer from among its members.

    (c)   The Congress may compel the attendance and testimony of witnesses and the production of documents or other matters before Congress or any of its committees.

Section 18. A majority of the members is a quorum, but a smaller number may adjourn from day to day and compel the attendance of absent members.

Section 19. The Congress shall keep and publish a journal of its proceedings. A roll call vote entered on the journal shall be taken at the request of 1/5 of the members present. Legislative proceedings shall be conducted in the English language. A member may use his own language if not fluent in English, and Congress shall provide translation.

Section 20. To become law, a bill must pass 2 readings on separate days. To pass first reading a 2/3 vote of all members is required. On final reading each state delegation shall cast one vote and a 2/3 vote of all the delegations is required. All votes shall be entered on the journal.

Section 21.

    (a)   The Congress may make no law except by statute and may enact no statute except by bill. The enacting clause of a bill is: "BE IT ENACTED BY THE CONGRESS OF THE FEDERATED STATES OF MICRONESIA:". A bill may embrace but one subject expressed in its title. A provision outside the subject expressed in the title is void.

(b)   A law may not be amended or revised by reference to its title only. The law as revised or section as amended shall be published and re-enacted at full length.

Section 22.   A bill passed by Congress shall be presented to the President for approval. If he disapproves of the bill, he shall return it with his objections to Congress within 10 days. If Congress has 10 or less days remaining in its session, or has adjourned he shall return the bill within 30 days after presentation. If the President does not return a bill within the appropriate period, it becomes law as if approved.

ARTICLE X: EXECUTIVE

Section 1.   The executive power of the national government is vested in the President of the Federated States of Micronesia. He is elected by Congress for a term of four years by a majority vote of all the members. He may not serve for more than 2 consecutive terms.

Section 2.   The following powers are expressly delegated to the President:

(a)   to faithfully execute and implement the provisions of this Constitution and all national laws;

(b)   to receive all ambassadors and to conduct foreign affairs and the national defense in accordance with national law;

(c)   to grant pardons and reprieves, except that the chief executive of each state shall have this power concurrently with respect to persons convicted under state law; and

(d)   with the advice and consent of Congress, to appoint ambassadors; all judges of the Supreme Court and other courts prescribed by statute; the principal officers of executive departments in the national government; and such other officers as may be provided for by statute. Ambassadors and principal officers serve at the pleasure of the President.

Section 3.   The President:

(a)   is head of state of the Federated States of Micronesia;

(b)   may make recommendations to Congress, and shall make an annual report to Congress on the state of the nation; and

(c)   shall perform such duties as may be provided by statute.

Section 4.   A person is ineligible to become President unless he is a member of Congress for a 4-year term, a citizen of the Federated States of Micronesia by birth, and a resident of the Federated States of Micronesia for at least 15 years.

Section 5.   After the election of the President, the Vice-President is elected in the same manner as the President, has the same qualifications, and serves for the same term of office.   He may not be a resident of the same state.   After the election of the President and the Vice-President, vacancies in Congress shall be declared.

Section 6.   If the office of the President is vacant, or the President is unable to perform his duties, the Vice-President becomes President.   The Congress shall provide by statute for the succession in the event both offices are vacant, or either or both officers are unable to discharge their duties.

Section 7.   The compensation of the President or Vice-President may not be increased or reduced during his term.   They may hold no other office and may receive no other compensation from the Federated States of Micronesia or from a state.

Section 8.   Executive departments shall be established by Statute.

Section 9.

(a)   If required to preserve public peace, health, or safety, at a time of extreme emergency caused by civil disturbance, natural disaster, or immediate threat of war, or insurrection, the President may declare a state of emergency and issue appropriate decrees.

(b)   A civil right may be impaired only to the extent actually required for the preservation of peace, health, or safety.   A declaration of emergency may not impair the power of the judiciary except that the declaration shall be free from judicial interference for 30 days after it is first issued.

(c)   Within 30 days after the declaration of emergency, the Congress of the Federated States of Micronesia shall convene at the call of its presiding officer or the President to consider revocation, amendment, or extension of the declaration. Unless it expires by its own terms, is revoked, or extended, a declaration of emergency is effective for 30 days.

ARTICLE XI: JUDICIAL

Section 1.   The judicial power of the national government is vested in a Supreme Court and inferior courts established by statute.

Section 2.   The Supreme Court is a court of record and the highest court in the nation. It consists of a Chief Justice and not more than 5 associate justices. Each justice is a member of both the trial division and the appellate division, except that sessions of the trial division may be held by one justice. No justice may sit with the appellate division in a case heard by him in the trial division. At least 3 justices shall hear and decide appeals. Decision is by a majority of those sitting.

Section 3.   The Chief Justice and associate justices of the Supreme Court are appointed by the President with the approval of 2/3 of Congress. Justices serve during good behavior.

Section 4.   If the Chief Justice is unable to perform his duties he shall appoint an associate justice to act in his stead. If the office is vacant, or the Chief Justice fails to make the appointment, the President shall appoint an associate justice to act as Chief Justice until the vacancy is filled or the Chief Justice resumes his duties.

Section 5.   The qualifications and compensation of justices and other judges may be prescribed by statute. Compensation of judges may not be diminished during their terms of office unless all salaries prescribed by statute are reduced by a uniform percentage.

Section 6

(a)   The trial division of the Supreme Court has
      original and exclusive jurisdiction in cases
      affecting officials of foreign governments,
      disputes between states, admiralty or maritime
      cases, and in cases in which the national
      government is a party except where an interest
      in land is at issue.

(b)   The national courts, including the trial divi-
      sion of the Supreme Court, have concurrent
      original jurisdiction in cases arising under
      this Constitution; national law or treaties;
      and in disputes between a state and a citizen
      of another state, between citizens of differ-
      ent states, and between a state or a citizen
      thereof, and a foreign state, citizen, or
      subject.

(c)   When jurisdiction is concurrent, the proper
      court may be prescribed by statute.

Section 7.   The appellate division of the Supreme
Court may review cases heard in the national courts, and
cases heard in state or local courts if they require interpretation of this Constitution, national law, or a
treaty.   If a state constitution permits, the appellate
division of the Supreme Court may review other cases on
appeal from the highest state court in which a decision
may be had.

Section 8.   When a case in a state or local court
involves a substantial question requiring the interpretation of the Constitution, national law, or a treaty,
on application of a party or on its own motion the court
shall certify the question to the appellate division of
the Supreme Court.   The appellate division of the Supreme
Court may decide the case or remand it for further proceedings.

Section 9.   The Chief Justice is the chief admin-
istrator of the national judicial system and may appoint
an administrative officer who is exempt from civil service.
The Chief Justice shall make and publish and may amend
rules governing national courts, and by rule may:

(a)   divide the inferior national courts and the
      trial division of the Supreme Court into geo-
      graphical or functional divisions;

(b)   assign judges among the divisions of a court and give special assignments to retired Supreme Court justices and judges of state and other courts;

(c)   establish rules of procedure and evidence;

(d)   govern the transfer of cases between state and national courts;

(e)   govern the admission to practice and discipline of attorneys and the retirement of judges; and

(f)   otherwise provide for the administration of the national judiciary.

Judicial rules may be amended by statute.

Section 10.   The Congress shall contribute to the financial support of state judicial systems and may provide other assistance.

Section 11.   Court decisions shall be consistent with this Constitution, Micronesian customs and traditions, and the social and geographical configuration of Micronesia.

ARTICLE XII: FINANCE

Section 1.

(a)   Public money raised or received by the national government shall be deposited in a General Fund or special funds within the National Treasury. Money may not be withdrawn from the General Fund or special funds except by law.

(b)   Foreign financial assistance received by the national government shall be deposited in a Foreign Assistance Fund. Except where a particular distribution is required by the terms or special nature of the assistance, each state shall receive a share equal to the share of the national government and to the share of every other state.

Section 2.

(a)   The President shall submit an annual budget to Congress at a time prescribed by statute. The budget shall contain a complete plan of proposed expenditures, anticipated revenues, and other money available to the national government for the next fiscal year, together with additional information that Congress may require. The Congress may alter the budget in any respect.

(b)   No appropriation bills, except those recommended by the President for immediate passage, or to cover the operating expenses of Congress, may be passed on final reading until the bill appropriating money for the budget has been enacted.

(c)   The President may item veto an appropriation in any bill passed by Congress, and the procedure in such case shall be the same as for disapproval of an entire bill by the President.

Section 3.

(a)   The Public Auditor is appointed by the President with the advice and consent of Congress. He serves for a term of 4 years and until a successor is confirmed.

(b)   The Public Auditor shall inspect and audit accounts in every branch, department, agency or statutory authority of the national government and in other public legal entities or nonprofit organizations receiving public funds from the national government. Additional duties may be prescribed by statute.

(c)   The Public Auditor shall be independent of administrative control except that he shall report at least once a year to Congress. His salary may not be reduced during his term of office.

(d)   The Congress may remove the Public Auditor from office for cause by 2/3 vote. In that event the Chief Justice shall appoint an acting Public Auditor until a successor is confirmed.

ARTICLE XIII: GENERAL PROVISIONS

Section 1.   The national government of the Federated States of Micronesia recognizes the right of the people to education, health care, and legal services and shall take every step reasonable and necessary to provide these services.

Section 2. Radioactive, toxic chemical, or other harmful substances may not be tested, stored, used, or disposed of within the jurisdiction of the Federated States of Micronesia without the express approval of the national government of the Federated States of Micronesia.

Section 3. It is the solemn obligation of the national and state governments to uphold the provisions of this Constitution and to advance the principles of unity upon which this Constitution is founded.

Section 4. A noncitizen, or a corporation not wholly owned by citizens, may not acquire title to land or waters in Micronesia.

Section 5. An agreement for the use of land for an indefinite term is prohibited. An existing agreement becomes void 5 years after the effective date of this Constitution. Within that time, a new agreement shall be concluded between the parties. When the national government is a party, it shall initiate negotiations.

Section 6. The national government of the Federated States of Micronesia shall seek renegotiation of any agreement for the use of land to which the Government of the United States of America is a party.

Section 7. On assuming office, all public officials shall take an oath to uphold, promote, and support the laws and the Constitution as prescribed by statute.

ARTICLE XIV: AMENDMENTS

Section 1. An amendment to this Constitution may be proposed by a constitutional convention, popular initiative, or Congress in a manner provided by law. A proposed amendment shall become a part of the Constitution when approved by 3/4 of the votes cast on that amendment in each of 3/4 of the states. If conflicting constitutional amendments submitted to the voters at the same election are approved, the amendment receiving the highest number of affirmative votes shall prevail to the extent of such conflict.

Section 2. At least every 10 years, Congress shall submit to the voters the question: "Shall there be a convention to revise or amend the Constitution?" If a majority of ballots cast upon the question is in the affirmative, delegates to the convention shall be chosen no later than the next regular election, unless Congress provides for the selection of delegates earlier at a special election.

ARTICLE XV: TRANSITION

<u>Section 1</u>.   A statute of the Trust Territory of the
Pacific Islands continues in effect except to the extent
it is inconsistent with this Constitution, or is amended
or repealed.   A writ, action, suit, proceeding, civil
or criminal liability, prosecution, judgment, sentence,
order, decree, appeal, cause of action, defense, contract, claim, demand, title, or right continues unaf-
fected except as modified in accordance with the provisions
of this Constitution.

 <u>Section 2</u>.   A right, obligation, liability,. or con-
tract of the Government of the Trust Territory of the
Pacific Islands is assumed by the Federated States of
Micronesia except to the extent it directly affects or
benefits a government of a District not ratifying this
Constitution.

 <u>Section 3</u>.   An interest in property held by the
Government of the Trust Territory of the Pacific Islands
is transferred to the Federated States of Micronesia for
retention or distribution in accordance with this Constitution.

 <u>Section 4</u>.   A local government and its agencies may
continue to exist even though its charter or powers are
inconsistent with this Constitution.   To promote an
orderly transition to the provisions of this Constitution,
and until state governments are established, Congress
shall provide for the resolution of inconsistencies between local government charters and powers, and this
Constitution.   This provision ceases to be effective 5
years after the effective date of this Constitution.

 <u>Section 5</u>.   The Congress may provide for a smooth
and orderly transition to government under this Constitution.

 <u>Section 6</u>.   In the first congressional election,
congressional districts are apportioned among the states
as follows: Kusaie - 1; Marianas - 2; Marshalls - 4;
Palau - 2; Ponape - 3; Truk - 5; Yap - 1.   If Kusaie is not
a state at the time of the first election, 4 members
shall be elected on the basis of population in Ponape.

ARTICLE XVI: EFFECTIVE DATE

<u>Section 1</u>.   This Constitution takes effect 1 year after

ratification unless the Congress of Micronesia by joint resolution specifies an earlier date. If a provision of this Constitution is held to be in fundamental conflict with the United Nations Charter or the Trusteeship Agreement between the United States of America and the United Nations, the provision does not become effective until the date of termination of the Trusteeship Agreement.

Appendix II
Report on Basic Compact
of Free Association*

The leadership of the Congress of Micronesia and its
Joint Committee on Future Status met with the President's
Personal Representative for Micronesian Status Negotiations on Saipan, Northern Mariana Islands, on May 28
through June 1, 1976. On June 2, 1976, the members of
the Joint Committee on Future Status of the Congress of
Micronesia and the President's Personal Representative
for Micronesian Status Negotiations met in plenary session. The working sessions and the plenary session
constituted the eighth round of talks on the future
political status of the Caroline and Marshall Islands.

The leadership of the Congress of Micronesia and
its Joint Committee on Future Status reaffirmed their
position that negotiations should proceed toward the
Congress of Micronesia's desired objective, a Compact
of Free Association between the United States and a
future Federated States of Micronesia. In working sessions, the Congress of Micronesia-Joint Committee on
Future Status Leadership and the President's Personal
Representative reviewed the October 1974 draft Compact
of Free Association. Suggested alterations to that
draft were then presented to the full Joint Committee on
Future Status for its consideration. Throughout this
review process, the leadership of the Congress of Micronesia
and its Joint Committee on Future Status reported to the
full Joint Committee on Future Status, to prospective members of the new Commission on Future Status and Transition, and also consulted with several leaders from the

---

*Reprinted by permission of Trust Territory Public
Information Division.

various districts and Micronesian members of the Trust Territory Administration.

During this review process both sides confirmed old understandings and reached new understandings and agreement on the basic principles and the text of the draft Compact of Free Association. These agreements confirmed that:

-Sovereignty resides in the people of Micronesia.

-The people of Micronesia have the sovereign right to choose their own future political status.

-The people of Micronesia will govern themselves under their own laws and under their own elected government. That government will have full responsibility for and authority over the internal affairs of Micronesia. That all land in Micronesia belongs to and is to be controlled by Micronesians.

-The people of Micronesia, through an exercise of their sovereign right of self-determination, will vest in the United States full responsibility for and authority over the foreign affairs and defense matters of Micronesia.

-The United States will provide financial assistance to the people of Micronesia in order to advance their economic and social welfare and in recognition of the special relationship that has existed and continues to exist between the United States and the people of Micronesia.

-The citizens of Micronesia will be given the privileges of a national of the United States in order to provide them freedom of travel, residence, and employment in the United States.

-The United States will have a resident representative in Micronesia for the purpose of maintaining close and regular consultations on matters of mutual interest. Micronesia will have a similar resident representative in Washington, D.C.

-Disputes relating to the interpretation or application of the provisions of the Compact will be resolved by good faith negotiations and if such negotiations do not result in a mutually satisfactory settlement within a reasonable period of time, the matter may be submitted to either the United States' courts or to arbitration for resolution.

-The Compact will be submitted for approval to the people of Micronesia in a plebiscite so that they can exercise their sovereign right of self-determination.

That the Compact will be approved by Micronesia if at least 55% of those voting in the plebiscite vote in favor of the Compact, including a majority in at least four of the six States of Micronesia.

-The Compact may be amended or terminated at any time by mutual consent. That after the expiration of the first fifteen years following its entry into force, the Compact may also be terminated unilaterally by either party. After that period of time, the Government of Micronesia may terminate the Compact unilaterally if a vote of the people of Micronesia has been taken in which at least 55% of the vote shall favor termination in at least two-thirds of the States of Micronesia.

Only one single area remains to be resolved before the Compact is put to the Congress of Micronesia and submitted to the people of Micronesia in a plebiscite. This one and only area is an important one to both Micronesia and the United States. Micronesia's great and legitimate interest in preserving and protecting Micronesian ocean resources for the full economic benefit of the people of Micronesia is recognized and shared by the United States. Law of the Sea matters of course have global significance and the United States has world-wide interests which also must be kept in mind.

The talks relating to Micronesia's marine resources and their future development were highly useful. Areas in need of further exploration were identified and are being given immediate attention by the United States Government. It was agreed that further exchanges between experts representing both parties on this complex matter will take place in the near future.

The agreements reached were publicly confirmed in a plenary session at which time the members of the Joint Committee on Future Status and the President's Personal Representative formally reviewed the draft Compact of Free Association and indicated their agreement with the Compact's language by initialling each of the Compact's twelve titles and three annexes.

Both delegations agreed that these talks were most successful in arriving at full agreement on arrangements which will provide for a future mutually beneficial close and enduring relationship of free association between the United States and the people of Micronesia. The completion of the negotiations toward the resolution of Micronesia's future political status, after many years of hard work, now is in sight.

Notes

1. The rain that falls on coral islands quickly per-
colates through the sand and cobbles and into the reef
that lies below. The reef, although porous, slows the
dissipation of the fresh water into the surrounding sea,
and because fresh water is less dense than salt water
(a ratio of 40:41), a "lens" of fresh water, technically
termed the Ghyben-Hertzberg lens, is formed. It rests
"floating" on the surface of the underlying seawater.

2. The accuracy of this date has been questioned since
it is based on analysis of shell materials using radiocarbon techniques of the 1950s.

3. Evans, Meggers, and Riesenberg (Radiocarbon 1965)
have obtained a radiocarbon date on Ponape that indicates
this island was settled by A.D. 1150.

4. Although in this matter Grace's conclusions (1961)
are similar to Dyen's (1965), there are significant differences of opinion between the two, especially relating
to reconstruction of Oceanic migrations. Nevertheless,
Dyen's conclusions, first that Palauan, Yapese, and
Chamorro are only distantly related to the other nuclear
Micronesian languages, and second, that these nuclear
Micronesian languages are branches (along with New
Hebridean, Rotuman, and Fijian) of the same subfamily,
are comparable to those of other linguists who have
worked with Micronesian languages.

5. The following works (listed in the bibliography) deal
specifically with the Chamorro and the Mariana Islands:
Bowers, 1951; Callander, 1768; Carano and Sanchez, 1964;
Costenoble, 1905; Emerick, 1958; Fritz, 1904; Joseph and

Murray, 1951: Pigafetta, 1874; Safford, 1902; Spoehr, 1951, 1952, 1954, 1957; Taylor, 1951; Thompson, 1945, 1947.

6.   There is also a sizable Carolinian minority population settled on Saipan and the Marianas to the north. These individuals are primarily descendants of migrants who moved to the Marianas from the central Caroline atolls between 1815 and 1900.   In 1969 the Carolinian population in the Marianas numbered approximately 2000 individuals.

7.   Throughout this essay the term *clan* is used to refer to a named unilinear, usually exogamous, nonlocalized descent group, the members of which claim (but are unable to trace genealogically) descent from a common ancestor. In some anthropological literature a distinction is drawn between clans (partilineal descent groups) and *sibs* (matrilineal descent groups), while in another case *clan* refers only to a kind of residential kin group (Murdock, 1949, pp. 65-78).   Even though in Micronesia the groups as defined above are universally matrilineal, I have chosen *clan* in preference to *sib* since the former is more commonly encountered in the literature (and hence is most familiar to the nonspecialist).

8.   The major anthropological works dealing with the people of Palau are as follows: Barnett, 1949, 1960; Cheyne, 1852; Force, 1960; Force and Force, 1965, 1972; Hidikata, 1973; Kaneshiro, 1958a; Keate, 1788; Krämer, 1917-1929; Kubary, 1885, 1889-1895; McKnight, 1960a, 1960b; Matsumura, 1918; Osborne, 1966; Shineberg, ed., 1971; Tetens, 1958; Useem, 1945, 1949, 1950; Yanaihara, 1940.

9.   Extensive changes in Palauan culture have occurred during the last ten years, but the number of Americans actually resident in these islands has never been more than a few hundred.

10.   Raymond Firth (1957, p. 5) has defined ambilaterality as a system ". . . in which, in any one generation, both kinds of parents are feasible for affiliation but some selectivity is possible, with difference of emphasis." In Polynesia, the area of Firth's concern, the ambilateral systems often have a patrilateral emphasis; in the Palauan case there is a decided matrilateral emphasis.   Roland and Maryanne Force (1972) feel, however, that traditionally

the Palauan descent system was strongly matrilineal and that the flexibility of the system (that is, ambilaterality) developed as a consequence of postcontact depopulation and acculturation.

11.   In Palauan these units are called *bital wa ma bital wa* (often shortened to *bitang ma bitang*).   McKnight (1960b) translates the former as "side-leg" but Force (1960)believes "other-leg" is a more accurate translation.

12.   This arrangement of even-numbered clans allied in opposition to odd-numbered ones is described by Force (1960, p. 37) and Force and Force (1972).   McKnight (1960b, pp. 68-70), however, describes the arrangement as one in which it was usual for the first, fourth, sixth, eighth, and tenth ranking clans to be in opposition to an alliance of second, third, fifth, seventh, and ninth ranks.

13.   In the Palauan orthography a glottal stop is rendered by *ch*.

14.   Major sources dealing with Yap and its people include the following: de Beauclair, 1963, 1967; Cheyne, 1852; Defngin, 1959; Furness, 1910; Gifford and Gifford, 1959; Hunt, Kidder, and Schneider, 1954; Kaneshiro, 1958b; Lingenfelter, 1975; Mahoney, 1958; Müller, 1917-1918; Salesius, 1906; Schneider, 1949, 1953, 1955, 1957a, 1957b, 1962; Shineberg, ed., 1971; Tetens, 1958; Underwood, 1969; Walleser, 1913.   Addenda: Labby, David, 1976, *The Demystification of Yap*. University of Chicago Press.

15.   Rumung and Map are districts formed by foreign administrators; traditionally they were part of Gagil district.

16.   Ethnographic details on various central Carolinian societies are included in the following works: Alkire, 1965, 1968, 1970; Burrows, 1952, 1963; Burrows and Spiro, 1953; Callander, 1768; Cantova, 1881; Damm, 1938; Damm and Sarfert, 1935; Eilers, 1936; Girschner, 1913; Gladwin, 1958, 1964, 1970; Hambruch, 1912; Hasebe, 1928; Kotzebue, 1821; Krämer, 1935, 1938; Lessa, 1950, 1955, 1961, 1966; Murphy, 1948, 1950; Riesenberg and Kaneshiro, 1960.

17.   Major ethnographic works on the people of Truk include the following: Bollig, 1927; Caughy, 1970; Efot, 1966; Finsch, 1888-1893, Vol. 6; A. Fischer, 1963; J.L. Fischer,

1956, 1958b; Fischer and Fischer, 1957; Gladwin, 1960;
Gladwin and Sarason, 1953; R. Goodenough, 1970; W. Good-
enough, 1949, 1951, 1953, 1956, 1964; Krämer, 1932; Le-
Bar, 1964; Mahony, 1960; Murdock and Goodenough, 1947;
Swartz, 1959, 1960.

18. Details of Ponapean culture and society may be
obtained from the following sources: Bascom, 1948,
1949, 1950, 1965; Cheyne, 1852; Christian, 1899; Eilers,
1934; Finsch, 1880, 1888-1893, Vol. 5; J.L. Fischer, 1956,
1958a, 1970; Fischer and Fischer, 1957; Garvin and Riesenberg, 1952; Hambruch, 1932; Hambruch and Eilers, 1936;
Hughes, 1969a; Kubary, 1874; Mahony and Lawrence, 1959;
Murrill, 1950; O'Connell, 1836; Riesenberg, 1948, 1950,
1959, 1965, 1968; Shineberg, ed., 1971.

19. In addition to Wilson (1968), other accounts deal-
ing with the people of Kusaie include Bliss, 1907;
Finsch, 1888-1893, Vol. 5; Fischer and Fischer, 1957;
Sarfert, 1919-1920.

20. Important publications on Marshallese life include
the following: Bliss, 1907; Davenport, 1960; Erdland,
1912, 1914; Finsch, 1888-1893, Vol. 5; Hambruch, 1912;
Kiste, 1968, 1974; Kotzebue, 1821; Krämer and Nevermann,
1938; MacKenzie, 1960; Mason, 1950, 1952, 1954; Mason
and Uyehara, 1953; Spoehr, 1949a, 1949b; Tobin, 1953,
1954, 1958, 1967; United Nations, 1954; Wedgwood, 1942/3.

21. Ethnographic details on the Gilbertese can be obtained from the following works: Catala, 1957; Finsch,
1888-1893, Vol. 4; Gilbert, 1789; Goodenough, 1955;
Grimble, 1921, 1931, 1933-1934, 1952, 1957; Hale, 1846;
Lambert, 1963, 1964, 1966, 1970; Lundsgaarde, 1966,
1968a, 1968b, 1970; Luomala, 1953; Maude, 1963; Maude
and Maude, 1931, 1932; Murdoch, 1923; Roberts, 1953;
Silverman, 1970; Stevenson, 1900.

22. Bernd Lambert (personal communication) states that
in the past on Butaritari and Makin, genealogies were
remembered for nine or more generations "so that experts
could trace supposed blood relationships connecting the
entire native-born population of Butaritari-Makin."

23. The major ethnographic works dealing with traditional

Nauru include Ellis, 1935; Hambruch, 1914-1915; Kayser, 1917-1918; Stephen, 1936; Wedgwood, 1936.

24. Sources that discuss modern political change in Micronesia include Heine, 1974; Hughes and Lingenfelter, 1974; Joint Committee on Future Status, 1972; Kiste, 1974; Mason, 1975; Office of Micronesian Status Negotiations, 1972; Viviani, 1970; and Wenkam and Baker, 1971.

Additional Sources

In addition to the bibliography by Utinomi (1952), an extensive listing for Micronesia may be obtained from C.R.H. Taylor, *A Pacific Bibliography* (Oxford University Press, 1965).

Libraries with significant holdings in Micronesian ethnography include the library and Pacific Scientific Information Center of the Bernice P. Bishop Museum, Honolulu; British National Library, London; Congress of Micronesia Library, Saipan; Library of Congress, Washington, D.C.; Micronesian Area Research Center Library, University of Guam; Micronesian Seminar Library, Xavier High School, Truk; and the University of Hawaii Library.

Professional journals that frequently publish articles on the peoples and cultures of Micronesia include *Ethnology, Journal of the Polynesian Society, Micronesica: Journal of the University of Guam, Journal of Pacific History,* and *Oceania.* Several popular publications cover current events in the area. Three of the best known are the *Micronesian Reporter*, Saipan (a monthly magazine); *The Marianas Variety*, Saipan (a weekly newspaper); and *The Micronesian Independent*, Majuro (a weekly newspaper).

Museums holding Micronesian collections include the Bernice P. Bishop Museum, Honolulu; British Museum, London; National Museum of Natural History, Smithsonian Institution, Washington, D.C.; Field Museum of Natural History, Chicago; Peabody Museum, Salem, Massachusetts; University of Illinois Museum, Urbana; University of Pennsylvania Museum; Oakland Public Museum, Oakland, California; and the National Museum of Ethnography, Osaka, Japan.

References*

Alkire, William H. (1960). "Cultural adaptation in the Caroline Islands." *Journal of the Polynesian Society,* Wellington, N.Z., 69: 123-150.

Alkire, William H. (1965). *Lamotrek Atoll and Inter-island Socioeconomic Ties.* Urbana: University of Illinois Press. Illinois Studies in Anthropology, No. 5.

Alkire, William H. (1968). "Porpoises and taro." *Ethnology,* 7: 280-289.

Alkire, William H. (1970). "Systems of measurement on Woleai Atoll, Caroline Islands." *Anthropos,* 65: 1-73.

Alkire, William H. (1974). "Land Tenure in the Woleai." In H. P. Lundsgaarde, Ed., *Land Tenure in Oceania,* pp. 39-69. Honolulu: University Press of Hawaii.

Arago, Jacques-Etienne V. (1823). *Narrative of a Voyage Round the World in 'Uranie' and 'Physicienne'* . . . 1817-1820, 2 vols. London: Treuttel and Wurtz.

Barnett, Homer (1949). *Palauan Society: a Study of Contemporary Native Life in the Palau Islands.* Eugene: University of Oregon Press.

Barnett, Homer (1960). *Being a Palauan.* New York: Holt.

Barrau, Jacques (1961). *Subsistence Agriculture in Polynesia and Micronesia.* Bishop Museum, Honolulu, Bulletin No. 223.

Bascom, W. R. (1948). "Ponapean prestige economy." *Southwestern Journal of Anthropology,* 4: 211-221.

Bascom, W. R. (1949). "Subsistence farming on Ponape." *New Zealand Geographer,* 5: 115-129.

Bascom, W. R. (1950). "Ponape: the tradition of retaliation." *Far Eastern Quarterly,* 10: 56-62.

---

*This bibliography does not include items published in Japanese since these sources are usually not available outside Japan.

Bascom, W. R. (1965). *Ponape: a Pacific Economy in Transition.* University of California Anthropological Records, No. 22.

Beauclair, Inez de (1963). "The stone money of Yap Island." *Bulletin of the Institute of Ethnology, Academia Sinica,* 16: 147-160.

Beauclair, Inez de (1963). "Ueber Religion und Magie auf Yap." *Sociologus,* 13: 68-84.

Beauclair, Inez de (1967). "On religion and mythology of Yap Island, Micronesia." *Bulletin of the Institute of Ethnology, Academia Sinica,* 23: 23-37.

Bentzen, C. (1949). *Land and Livelihood on Mokil.* Washington, D.C.: Pacific Science Board. Coordinated Investigation of Micronesian Anthropology, No. 25.

Bliss, Theodora C. (1907). *Micronesia. Fifty Years in the Islands World: a History of the Mission of the American Board.* Boston: American Board for Foreign Missions.

Bollig, Laurentius (1927). *Die Bewohner der Truk-Inseln: Religion, Leben und kurze Grammatik eines Mikronesiervolkes.* Münster, Germany: Anthropos Bibliothek.

Bowers, Neal M. (1951). *Problems of Resettlement of Saipan, Tinian and Rota, Mariana Islands.* Unpublished Ph.D. thesis. University of Michigan.

Bryan, E.H., Jr., and staff (1970). *Land in Micronesia and Its Resources: an Annotated Bibliography.* Bishop Museum, Honolulu, Pacific Scientific Information Center.

Buck, Peter (1938). *Vikings of the Sunrise.* Philadelphia: Lippincott.

Burrows, E.G. (1952). "From value to ethos on Ifaluk Atoll." *Southwestern Journal of Anthropology,* 8: 13-36.

Burrows, E.G. (1963). *Flower in My Ear.* Seattle: University of Washington Press.

Burrows, E.G., and M.E. Spiro (1953). *An Atoll Culture: Ethnography of Ifaluk in the Central Carolines.* New Haven, Conn.: Human Relations Area Files Press.

Callander, John (1768). *Terra Australis Cognita: or, Voyages to the Terra Australis, or Southern Hemisphere during the Sixteenth, Seventeenth and Eighteenth Centuries,* Vol. 3., pp. 9-56. Edinburgh: Donaldson.

Cantova, J.A., S.J. (1881). *Descubbrimiento y Descripcion de las Islas Garbanzos.* Madrid (?): F. Carrasco.

Carano, Paul, and P.C. Sanchez (1964). *A Complete History of Guam.* Rutland, Vt.: Tuttle.

Catala, René (1957). *Report on the Gilbert Islands.* Pacific Science Board, Atoll Research Bull. No. 59.

Caughey, John (1970). *Cultural Values in a Micronesian Society*. Unpublished Ph.D. thesis, University of Pennsylvania.

Chang, Kwang-chih, George W. Grace, and W. G. Solheim II (1969). "Movement of the Malayo-Polynesians." *Current Anthropology*, 5: 359-406.

Chapman, Peter (1964). *Micronesian Archaeology: an Annotated Bibliography*. Unpublished M.A. thesis, Stanford University.

Cheyne, Andrew (1852). *A Description of Islands in the Western Pacific Ocean . . . Manners and Customs . . . and Vocabularies*. London: Potter.

Choris, Louis (1822). *Voyage Pittoresque autour du Monde, avec des Portraits de Sauvages . . . .* Paris: Didot.

Christian, F.W. (1899). *The Caroline Islands*. London: Methuen.

Costenoble, H.H. (1905). "Die Marianen." *Globus*, 88: 4-9, 72-81, 92-94.

Damm, Hans (1938). *Zentralkarolinen*, Part 2. Hamburg: De Gruyter. (See Thilenius, 1913-1938.)

Damm, Hans, and E. Sarfert (1935). *Inseln um Truk*, Vol. 2. Hamburg: De Gruyter. (See Thilenius, 1913-1938.)

Darwin, Charles (1901). *The Structure and Distribution of Coral Reefs*, 3rd ed. New York: Appleton.

Davenport, William (1960). "Marshall Islands navigational charts." *Imago Mundi*, 15: 19-26.

Defngin, F. (1959). "Yam cultivation in Yap." *Anthropological Working Papers* (Trust Territory Government, Guam), 4: 38-65.

de Young, John, Ed. (1958). *Trust Territory Land Tenure Handbook*. Guam: Trust Territory Government.

Dyen, Isadore (1949). "On the history of the Trukese vowels." *Language*, 25: 420-436.

Dyen, Isadore (1965). *A Lexicostatistical Classification of the Austronesian Languages*. International Journal of American Linguistics, Memoir No. 19. Indiana University Publications in Anthropology and Linguistics.

Efot, Boutau K. (1966). "The tale of Pupily-Eyeballs-Thing: a Truk ghost story" (transl. W. Goodenough). *Expedition*, 8: 23-29.

Eilers, Anneliese (1934). *Inseln um Ponape*. Hamburg: De Gruyter. (See Thilenius, 1913-1938.)

Eilers, Anneliese (1936). *Westkarolinen*, Parts 1 and 2. Hamburg: De Gruyter. (See Thilenius, 1913-1938.)

Ellis, Albert F. (1935). *Ocean Island and Nauru: Their Story*. Sydney: Angus and Robertson.

Embree, J.F. (1948). "Kickball and some other parallels between Siam and Micronesia." *Journal of the Siam Society*, 37: 33-38.

Emerick, R.G. (1958). "Land tenure in the Marianas." In John de Young, Ed., *Land Tenure Patterns, Trust Territory of the Pacific Islands*, pp. 217-250. Guam: Trust Territory Government.

Erdland, August (1912). "Die Eingeborenen der Marshall-Inseln im Verkehr mit ihren Häuptlingen." *Anthropos*, 7: 559-565.

Erdland, August (1914). *Die Marshall-Insulaner. Leben und Sitte, Sinn und Religion eines Südseevolkes*. Münster: Ethnologische-Anthropos Bibliothek.

Finney, B.R. (1965). "Polynesian peasants and proletarians." *Journal of the Polynesian Society*, 74: 269-328.

Finsch, O. (1880). "Ueber die Bewohner von Ponape." *Zeitschrift für Ethnologie*, 12: 301-332.

Finsch, O. (1888-1893). *Ethnologische Erfahrungen und Belegstücke aus der Südsee*, Vols. 4, 5, 6. Vienna: Annalen des K. K. Naturhistorie Hofmuseums.

Firth, Raymond (1957). "A note on descent groups in Polynesia." *Man*, 57: 4-7.

Fischer. A.M. (1963). "Reproduction in Truk." *Ethnology*, 2: 526-540.

Fischer, J.L. (1956). "The position of men and women in Truk and Ponape: a comparative analysis. Comparisons of kinship terminology and folktales." *Journal of American Folklore*, 69: 55-62.

Fischer, J.L. (1958a). "Contemporary Ponape land tenure." In John de Young, Ed., *Land Tenure Patterns, Trust Territory of the Pacific Islands*, pp. 77-160. Guam: Trust Territory Government.

Fischer, J.L. (1958b). "Native land tenure in the Truk district." In John de Young, Ed., *Land Tenure Patterns, Trust Territory of the Pacific Islands*, pp. 161-215. Guam: Trust Territory Government.

Fischer, J.L. (1970). "Adoption on Ponape." In V. Carroll, Ed., *Adoption in Eastern Oceania*, pp. 292-313. Honolulu: University of Hawaii Press.

Fischer, J.L., with the assistance of A.M. Fischer (1957). *The Eastern Carolines*. New Haven, Conn.: Human Relations Area Files Press. Behavior Science Monographs.

Force, Roland W. (1960). *Leadership and Cultural Change in Palau*. Chicago Natural History Museum, Fieldiana Anthropology, Vol. 50.

Force, Roland W., and Maryanne Force (1965). "Political change in Micronesia." In R. W. Force, Ed., *Induced Political Change in the Pacific*, pp. 1-16. Honolulu: Bishop Museum Press.

Force, Roland W., and Maryanne Force (1972). *Just One House: a Description and Analysis of Kinship in the Palau Islands*. Bishop Museum, Honolulu, Bulletin No. 235.

Freemen, O.W. (1951). *Geography of the Pacific*, Chapters 8, 9, 10. New York: Wiley.

Fritz, Georg (1904). "Die Chamorro, eine Geschichte und Ethnographie der Marianen." *Ethnologisches Notizblatt*, 3: 25-100.

Furness, William H. (1910). *The Island of Stone Money, Yap of the Carolines*. Philadelphia: Lippincott.

Garvin, Paul L., and S.H. Riesenberg (1952). "Respect behavior on Ponape." *American Anthropologist*, 54: 201-221.

Geographical Handbook (1945). *Pacific Islands: Western Pacific*, Vol. 4. U.K. Government, Naval Intelligence Division.

Gifford, E.W., and D.S. Gifford (1959). *Archaeological Excavations in Yap.* Anthropological Records, Vol. 18, No. 2, University of California.

Gilbert, Thomas (1789). *Voyage from N.S.W. to Canton in . . . 1788*. London: Debrett

Girschner, Max (1913). "Die Karolineninsel Namoluk und ihrer Bewohner." *Baessler-Archiv*, 2: 123-215; 3: 165-190.

Gladwin, Thomas (1958). "Canoe travel in the Truk area." *American Anthropologist*, 60: 893-899.

Gladwin, Thomas (1960). "Petrus Mailo, Chief of Moen." In J. Casagrande, Ed., In the *Company of Man*, pp. 41-62. New York: Harper.

Gladwin, Thomas (1964). "Culture and logical process." In W. Goodenough, Ed., *Explorations in Cultural Anthropology*, pp. 167-177. New York: McGraw-Hill.

Gladwin, Thomas (1970). *East Is a Big Bird*. Cambridge, Mass.: Harvard University Press.

Gladwin, Thomas, and S.B. Sarason (1953). *Truk: Man in Paradise*. New York: Viking Fund Publication No. 20.

Goodenough, Ruth G. (1970). "Adoption on Romonum, Truk." In V. Carroll, Ed., *Adoption in Eastern Oceania*, pp. 314-340. Honolulu: University of Hawaii Press.

Goodenough, Ward (1949). "Premarital freedom on Truk: theory and practice." *American Anthropologist*, 51: 615-620.

Goodenough, Ward (1951). *Property, Kin and Community on Truk*. Yale University Publications in Anthropology, No. 46.

Goodenough, Ward (1953). *Native Astronomy in the Central Carolines*. Philadelphia: University of Pennsylvania Press.

Goodenough, Ward (1955). "A problem in Malayo-Polynesian social organization." *American Anthropologist*, 57: 71-83.

Goodenough, Ward (1956). "Residence rules." *Southwestern Journal of Anthropology*, 12: 22-37.

Goodenough, Ward (1964). "Property and language on Truk." In D. Hymes, Ed., *Language in Culture and Society*, pp. 185-188. New York: Harper and Row.

Grace, George (1961). "Austronesian linguistics and culture history." *American Anthropologist*, 63: 359-368.

Grimble, Sir Arthur (1921). "From birth to death in the Gilbert Islands." *Journal of the Royal Anthropological Institute*, 51: 25-54.

Grimble, Sir Arthur (1931). "Gilbertese astronomy and astronomical observations." *Journal of the Polynesian Society*, 40: 197-224.

Grimble, Sir Arthur (1933-1934). "The migrations of the pandanus people." *Journal of the Polynesian Society*, Volumes 42/43. 112 pp.

Grimble, Sir Arthur (1952). *We Chose the Islands*. New York: Morrow.

Grimble, Sir Arthur (1957). *Return to the Islands*. London: Murray.

Grimble, Sir Arthur (1972). *Migration, Myth, and Magic from the Gilbert Islands*. Arranged and illustrated by Rosemary Grimble. London: Routledge and Kegan Paul.

Haddon, A.C., and J. Hornell (1936). *The Canoes of Polynesia, Fiji and Micronesia* (Canoes of Oceania, Vol. 1). Bishop Museum, Honolulu, Special Publication No. 27.

Hale, Horatio (1846). *United States Exploring Expedition . . . 1838-42 . . . Ethnography and Philology*. Philadelphia: Lea and Blanchard.

Hambruch, Paul (1912). *Die Schiffahrt auf den Karolinen und Marshall-Inseln*. Sammlung Meereskunde Vol. 6, No. 6. Berlin.

Hambruch, Paul (1914-1915). *Nauru*, 2 Vols. Hamburg: De Gruyter. (See Thilenius, 1913-1938.)

Hambruch, Paul (1932). *Ponape*, Part 1. Hamburg: De Gruyter. (See Thilenius, 1913-1938.)

Hambruch, Paul, and A. Eilers (1936). *Ponape*, Part 2. Hamburg: De Gruyter. (See Thilenius, 1913-1938.)

Handbuch Südsee (1913). *Die Karolinen, Marshall-Inseln und Marianen*. Berlin: Mittler.

Hasebe, Kotondo (1928). "On the islanders of Togobei (Nevel's Island)." *Journal of the Anthropological Society of Tokyo*, 43: 67-70.

Heine, Carl (1974). *Micronesia at the Crossroads: A reappraisal of the Micronesian Political Dilemma*. Honolulu: University Press of Hawaii.

Hidikata, Hisakatsu (1973). "Palauan Kinship." *Micronesian Area Research Center Publication, Number 1*. Guam: University of Guam. (Originally published in Japanese in *Kagaku Nanyo*, April 1940.)

Howells, William (1973). *The Pacific Islanders*. New York: Charles Scribner's Sons.

Hughes, Daniel T. (1969a). "Conflict and harmony: roles of councilman and section chief on Ponape." *Oceania*, 40: 32-41.

Hughes, Daniel T. (1969b). "Democracy in a traditional society: two hypotheses on role." *American Anthropologist*, 71: 36-45.

Hughes, Daniel and Sherwood Lingenfelter (1974). *Political Development in Micronesia*. Columbus: Ohio University Press.

Hunt, E.E. (1950). "A view of somatology and serology in Micronesia." *American Journal of Physical Anthropology*, 8: 157-184.

Hunt, E.E., N.R. Kidder, and D.M. Schneider (1954). "The depopulation of Yap." *Human Biology*, 26: 21-52.

Joint Committee on Future Status (1972). *Draft Compact of Free Association: The Fifth Round of Negotiation Held in Washington, D.C.* Saipan: Congress of Micronesia.

Joseph, Alice, and Veronica Murray (1951). *Chamorros and Carolineans of Saipan*. Cambridge, Mass.: Harvard University Press.

Kaneshiro, Shigeru (1958a). "Land tenure in the Palau Islands." In John de Young, Ed., *Land Tenure Patterns, Trust Territory of the Pacific Islands*, pp. 289-336. Guam: Trust Territory Government.

Kaneshiro, Shigeru (1958b). "Notes on Yap." (Mimeo.) University of Hawaii Interdepartmental Seminar.

Kayser, A. (1917-1918). "Die Eingeborenen von Nauru (Südsee)." *Anthropos*, 12/13: 313-337.

Keate, George (1788). *An Account of the Pelew Islands
. . . from Journals . . . of Capt. Henry Wilson, 1783.*
London: Wilson and Nichol.

Kiste, Robert (1968). *Kili Island: a Study of the Relocation of the Ex-Bikini Marshallese.* Department of
Anthropology, University of Oregon, Eugene.

Kiste, Robert (1974). *The Bikinians.* Menlo Park, California: Cummings.

Knudson, K.E. (1970). *Resource Fluctuation, Productivity,
and Social Organization on Micronesian Coral Islands.*
Unpublished Ph.D. thesis, University of Oregon.

Kotzebue, Otto von (1821). *Voyage of Discovery in the
South Sea . . . 1815, 16, 17, and 18, in the Ship
Rurick.* London: Phillips.

Krämer, Augustin (1906). *Hawaii, Ostmikronesien und
Samoa.* Stuttgart: Strecker und Schroeder.

Krämer, Augustin (1917-1929). *Palau,* Vol. 3, 4 parts.
Hamburg: De Gruyter. (See Thilenius, 1913-1938.)

Krämer, Augustin (1932). *Truk.* Hamburg: De Gruyter.
(See Thilenius, 1913-1938.)

Krämer, Augustin (1935). *Inseln um Truk,* Vol. 1. Hamburg: De Gruyter. (See Thilenius, 1913-1938.)

Krämer, Augustin (1938). *Zentralkarolinen,* Part 1. Hamburg: De Gruyter. (See Thilenius, 1913-1938.)

Krämer, Augustin, and Hans Nevermann (1938). *Ralik-Ratak
(Marshall Inseln).* Hamburg: De Gruyter. (See Thilenius,
1913-1938.)

Krieger, H.W. (1943). *Island Peoples of the Western
Pacific: Micronesia and Melanesia.* Washington, D.C.:
Smithsonian Institution.

Kubary, J.S. (1874). "Die Ruinen von Nan Matal auf der
Insel Ponape." *Journal des Museum Godeffroy,* 3: 123-
131.

Kubary, J.S. (1885). *Ethnographische Beiträge zur Kenntniss der Karolinischen Insel-Gruppe und Nachbarschaft.*
Berlin: Asher.

Kubary, J.S. (1889-1895). *Ethnographische Beiträge zur
Kenntniss des Karolinen Archipels.* Leiden: Trap.

Lambert, Bernd (1963). *Rank and Ramage in the Northern
Gilbert Islands.* Unpublished Ph.D. thesis, University
of California, Berkeley.

Lambert, Bernd (1964). "Fosterage in the Northern Gilbert Islands." *Ethnology,* 3: 232-258.

Lambert, Bernd (1966). "Ambilineal descent groups in
the Northern Gilbert Islands." *American Anthropologist,*
68: 641-664.

Lambert, Bernd (1970). "Adoption, guardianship, and social stratification in the Northern Gilbert Islands." In V. Carroll, Ed., *Adoption in Eastern Oceania*, pp. 261-291. Honolulu: University of Hawaii Press.

Lambert, Bernd (1971). "The Gilbert Islands: Micro-individualism." In R. Crocombe, Ed., *Land Tenure in the Pacific*, pp. 146-171. Oxford.

LeBar, F.M. (1964). *Trukese Material Culture*. Yale University Publications in Anthropology, No. 68.

Lessa, William A. (1950). "Ulithi and the outer native world." *American Anthropologist*, 52: 27-52.

Lessa, William A. (1955). "Depopulation on Ulithi." *Human Biology*, 27: 161-183.

Lessa, William A. (1961). *Tales from Ulithi Atoll*. Berkeley: University of California Press.

Lessa, William A. (1962). "An evaluation of early descriptions of Carolinian culture." *Ethnohistory*, 9: 313-404.

Lessa, William A. (1966). *Ulithi: a Micronesian Design for Living*. New York: Holt.

Lieber, Michael (1974). "Land Tenure on Kapingamarangi." In H. P. Lundesgaarde, Ed., *Land Tenure in Oceania*, pp. 70-99. Honolulu: University Press of Hawaii.

Lingenfelter, Sherwood G. (1975). *Yap: Political Leadership and Culture Change in an Island Society*. Honolulu: University Press of Hawaii.

Lundsgaarde, Henry P. (1966). *Cultural Adaptation in the Southern Gilbert Islands*. Unpublished Ph.D. thesis, University of Wisconsin.

Lundsgaarde, Henry P. (1968a). "The strategy and etiology of Gilbertese property disputes." *American Anthropologist*, 70: 86-93.

Lundsgaarde, Henry P. (1968b). "Some transformations in Gilbertese law, 1892-1966." *Journal of Pacific History*, 3: 117-130.

Lundsgaarde, Henry P. (1970). "Some legal aspects of Gilbertese adoption." In V. Carroll, Ed., *Adoption in Eastern Oceania*, pp. 236-260. Honolulu: University of Hawaii Press.

Lundsgaarde, Henry P. (1974). "The Evolution of Tenure Principles on Tamana Island, Gilbert Islands." In H. P. Lundsgaarde, Ed., *Land Tenure in Oceania*, pp. 179-214. Honolulu: University Press of Hawaii.

Luomala, Katherine (1949). "Micronesian mythology." *Dictionary of Folklore, Mythology and Legend*, 2: 717-722.

Luomala, Katherine (1953). *Ethnobotany of the Gilbert Islands*. Bishop Museum, Honolulu, Bulletin No. 213.

Lütke, Frédéric (1835). *Voyage autour du Monde Exécuté par Ordre de sa Majesté l'Empereur Nicholaus sur la Corvette 'Le Seniavine.'* Paris: Altas.

Mackenzie, J. Boyd (1960). "Breadfruit cultivation practices and beliefs in the Marshall Islands." *Anthropological Working Papers* (Trust Territory Government, Guam), 8.

McGrath, W.A. and W.S. Wilson (1971). "The Marshall, Caroline, and Mariana Islands: Too many foreign precedents." In R. Crocombe, Ed., *Land Tenure in the Pacific*, pp. 172-191. Oxford.

McKnight, R.K. (1960a). "Breadfruit cultivation practices and beliefs in Palau." *Anthropological Working Papers* (Trust Territory Government, Guam), 6: 1-47.

McKnight, R.K. (1960b). *Competition in Palau*. Unpublished Ph.D. thesis, Ohio State University.

Mahoney, Francis (1958). "Land tenure patterns on Yap island." In John de Young, Ed., *Land Tenure Patterns, Trust Territory of the Pacific Islands*, pp. 251-287. Guam: Trust Territory Government.

Mahony, Frank (1960). "The invention of a savings system in Truk." *American Anthropologist*, 62: 465-482.

Mahony, Frank, and P. Lawrence (1959). "Yam cultivation in Ponape." *Anthropological Working Papers* (Trust Territory Government, Guam), 4: 1-13.

Marshall, K.M. (1972). *The Structure of Solidarity and Alliance on Namoluk Atoll*. Unpublished Ph.D. thesis, University of Washington, Seattle.

Mason, Leonard (1950). "The Bikinians: a transplanted population." *Human Organization*, 9: 5-15.

Mason, Leonard (1952). *Anthropology-Geography Study of Arno Atoll, Marshall Islands*. Atoll Research Bulletin No. 10.

Mason, Leonard (1954). *Relocation of the Bikini Marshallese: a Study in Group Migration*. Unpublished Ph.D. thesis, Yale University.

Mason, Leonard (1959). "Suprafamilial authority and economic process in Micronesian atolls." *Humanités*, 95: 87-118. (Reprinted in A.P. Vayda, Ed., *Peoples and Cultures of the Pacific*, pp. 299-329. New York: Natural History Press.)

Mason, Leonard (1964). "Micronesia. Micronesia culture (art)." *Encyclopedia of World Art*, 9: 915-918, 918-930. New York: McGraw-Hill.

Mason, Leonard (1968). "The ethnology of Micronesia."
In A.P. Vayda, Ed., *Peoples and Cultures of the Pacific*,
pp. 275-298. New York: Natural History Press.

Mason, Leonard (1975). "The Many Faces of Micronesia."
Pacific Asian Studies 1: 5-37. Guam.

Mason, Leonard, and H. Uyehara (1953). "A quantitative
study of certain aspects of the man-land relationship
in Marshallese economy at Arno island." *Atoll Research Bulletin*, 17: 116-121.

Matsumura, Akira (1918). "Contributions to the ethnography of Micronesia." *College of Science Tokyo
Imperial University Journal*, 40: 1-174.

Matthews, W.K. (1951). "Characteristics of Micronesian."
Lingua (Amsterdam), 2: 419-437.

Maude, H.E. (1963). "The evolution of the Gilbertese
boti: an ethnohistorical interpretation." *Journal
of the Polynesian society*, 72. Supplement, Memoir No.
35.

Maude, H.E., and H.C. Maude (1931). "Adoption in the
Gilbert Islands." *Journal of the Polynesian Society*,
40: 225-235.

Maude, H.E., and H.C. Maude (1932). "The social organization of Banaba or Ocean Island, Central Pacific."
Journal of the Polynesian Society, 41: 262-301.

Müller-Wismar, Wilhelm (1917-1918). *Jap*, 2 vols. Hamburg: Friederichsen. (See Thilenius, 1913-1938.)

Munoz Barreda, V. (1894). *La Micronesia Española o las
Archipielagos de Marianas, Palaos y Carolinas*. Manila:
Amigos del Pais. (First edition 1792.)

Murai, Mary (1954). *Nutrition Study in Micronesia*.
Atoll Research Bulletin No. 27.

Murdoch, G.M. (1923). "Gilbert Islands weapons and
armour." *Journal of the Polynesian Society*, 32: 174-175.

Murdock, George P. (1948). "Anthropology in Micronesia."
New York Academy of Sciences Transactions 2: 9-16.

Murdock, George P. (1949). *Social Structure*. New York:
Macmillan.

Murdock, George P., and Ward Goodenough (1947). "Social
organization of Truk." *Southwestern Journal of Anthropology*, 3: 331-343.

Murphy, R.E. (1948). "Landownership on a Micronesian
atoll." *Geographical Review*, 38: 598-614.

Murphy, R.E. (1949). "'High' and 'low' islands in the
Eastern Carolines." *Geographical Review*, 39: 425-439.

Murphy, R.E. (1950). "Economic geography of a Micronesian atoll." *Annals of the Association of American
Geographers*, 40: 58-83.

Murrill, Rupert I. (1950). "Vital statistics of Ponape island, Eastern Carolines." *American Journal of Physical Anthropology*, 8: 185-194.

O'Connell, James F. (1836). *A Residence of Eleven Years in New Holland and the Caroline Islands . . .* Ed. B.B. Mussey. Boston: Mussey. (See Riesenberg, 1959.)

Office of Micronesian Status Negotiations (1972). *Marianas Political Status Negotiations*. Washington, D.C.

Oliver, Douglas (1951). *The Pacific Islands*. Cambridge, Mass.: Harvard University Press.

Oliver, Douglas, Ed. (1951). *Planning Micronesia's Future: a Summary of the U.S. Commercial Company's Economic Survey of Micronesia*. Cambridge, Mass.: Harvard University Press. (Reprinted 1971, University of Hawaii Press, Honolulu.)

Osborne, Douglas (1966). *The Archaeology of the Palau Islands: an Intensive Survey*. Bishop Museum, Honolulu, Bulletin No. 230.

Pacific Daily News (August 22, 1975). "Ponapean Proposes 'Chamber of Chiefs'," p. 6. Agana, Guam.

Pigafetta, Antonio (1874). *The First Voyage Round the World by Magellan,* Ed. Lord Stanley Alderley, p. 8. London: Hakluyt Society.

Pollock, Nancy (1974). "Landholding on Namu Atoll, Marshall Islands." In H.P. Lundsgaarde, Ed., *Land Tenure in Oceania*, pp. 100-129. Honolulu: University Press of Hawaii.

Radiocarbon (1965). "Ponape Series." *American Journal of Sciences*, 7: 253-254.

Richard, Dorothy (1957). *United States Naval Administration of the Trust Territory of the Pacific Islands,* 3 vols. Washington, D.C.: U.S. Office of Naval Operations.

Riesenberg, Saul H. (1948). "Magic and medicine in Ponape." *Southwestern Journal of Anthropology,* 4: 406-429.

Riesenberg, Saul H. (1950). *The Cultural Position of Ponape in Oceania*. Unpublished Ph.D. thesis, University of California, Berkeley.

Riesenberg, Saul H. (1959). "A Pacific voyager's hoax." *Ethnohistory*, 6: 238-264. (See O'Connell, 1836.)

Riesenberg, Saul H. (1965). "Table of voyages affecting Micronesian islands." *Oceania*, 36: 155-170.

Riesenberg, Saul H. (1968). *The Native Polity of Ponape*. Washington, D.C.: Smithsonian Contributions to Anthropology, Vol. 10.

Riesenberg, Saul H., and A.H. Gayton (1952). "Caroline Island belt weaving." *Southwestern Journal of Anthropology*, 8: 342-375.

Riesenberg, Saul H., and S. Kaneshiro (1960). *A Caroline Islands Script*. Bureau of American Ethnology, Bulletin No. 173.

Roberts, R.G. (1953). "The dynasty of Abemama." *Journal of the Polynesian Society*, 62: 267-278.

Safford, W.E. (1902). "Guam and its people." *American Anthropologist*, 4: 707-729.

Salesius, P. (1906). *Die Karolineninsel Yap* . . . Berlin: Süsserott.

Sarfert, E. (1919-1920). *Kusae* 2 vols. Hamburg: Friederichsen. (See Thilenius, 1913-1938.)

Schmeltz, J.D.E., and R. Krause (1881). *Die Ethnographisch-Anthropologische Abtheilung des Museum Godeffroy in Hamburg: ein Beitrag zur Kenntnis der Südsee-Völker*. Hamburg: Friederichsen.

Schneider, David (1949). *The Kinship System and Village Organization of Yap, West Caroline Islands, Micronesia: a Structural and Functional Account*. Unpublished Ph.D. thesis, Harvard University.

Schneider, David (1953). "Yap kinship terminology and kin groups." *American Anthropologist*, 55: 215-236.

Schneider, David (1955). "Abortion and depopulation on a Pacific island; Yap." In B.D. Paul, Ed., *Health, Culture, and Community*, pp. 211-235. New York: Russell Sage.

Schneider, David (1957a). "Political organization, supernatural sanctions and the punishment for incest on Yap." *American Anthropologist*, 59: 791-800.

Schneider, David (1957b). "Typhoons and Yap." *Human Organization*, 16: 10-15.

Schneider, David (1962). "Double descent on Yap." *Journal of the Polynesian Society*, 71: 1-24.

Shineberg, Dorothy, Ed. (1971). *The Trading Voyages of Andrew Cheyne, 1841-1844*. Honolulu: University of Hawaii Press.

Shutler, Richard, Jr., and M.E. Shutler (1975). *Oceanic Prehistory*. Menlo Park, California: Cummings.

Silverman, Martin (1970). "Banaban adoption." In V. Carroll, Ed., *Adoption of Eastern Oceania*, pp. 209-235. Honolulu: University of Hawaii Press.

Simmons, R.T., J.J. Graydon, D.C. Gadjusek, and P. Brown (1965). "Blood group genetic variations in natives in the Caroline Islands and other parts of Micronesia." *Oceania*, 36: 132-170.

Smith, J. Jerome (1973). "Land Tenure on Rota: Yester-
    day, today and tomorrow." *Association for Anthropology
    in Micronesia Newsletter*, 2(2): 9-12. Guam: Micro-
    nesian Area Research Center.
Spoehr, Alexander (1949a). *Majuro: a Village in the
    Marshall Islands*. Chicago Natural History Museum,
    Fieldiana Anthropology, Vol. 39.
Spoehr, Alexander (1949b). "The generation type kinship
    terminology in the Marshall and Gilbert Islands."
    Southwestern Journal of Anthropology, 5: 107-116.
Spoehr, Alexander (1951). "The Tinian Chamorros."
    Human Organization, 10(4): 16-20.
Spoehr, Alexander (1952). "Time perspective in Micro-
    nesia and Polynesia." *Southwestern Journal of Anthro-
    pology*, 8: 457-465.
Spoehr, Alexander (1954). *Saipan: the Ethnology of a
    War-Devastated Island*. Chicago Natural History Museum,
    Fieldiana Anthropology, Vol. 41.
Spoehr, Alexander (1957). *Marianas Prehistory: Archaeo-
    logical Survey and Excavations on Saipan, Tinian, and
    Rota*. Chicago Natural History Museum, Fieldiana
    Anthropology, Vol. 48.
Stephen, Ernest (1936). "Notes on Nauru." *Oceania*,
    7: 34-63.
Stevenson, Robert Louis (1900). *In the South Seas . . .*
    London: Chatto and Windus.
Stillfried, Bernhard (1953). *Die Soziale Organisation in
    Mikronesien*. Acta Ethnologica et Linguistica, Vienna, No.4.
Swartz, Marc J. (1959). "Leadership and status conflict
    on Romonum, Truk." *Southwestern Journal of Anthro-
    pology*, 15: 213-218.
Swartz, Marc J. (1960). "Situational determinants of
    kinship terminology." *Southwestern Journal of Anthro-
    pology*, 16: 393-397.
Taylor, J.L. (1951). "Saipan: a study in land utiliza-
    tion." *Economic Geography*, 27: 340-347.
Tetens, Alfred (1958). *Among the Savages of the South
    Seas: Memoirs of Micronesia, 1862-68,* transl. F.M.
    Spoehr. Stanford: Stanford University Press.
Thilenius, George, Ed. (1913-1938). *Ergebnisse der
    Südsee-Expedition, 1908-1910, Part 2, B, Mikronesien*
    (12 vols. in 25 parts). Hamburg: De Gruyter.
Thomas, W.L., Jr. (1967). "The Pacific basin: an
    introduction." In Herman R. Friis, Ed., *The Pacific
    Basin: a History of its Geographical Exploration*.
    New York: American Geographical Society.

Thompson, Laura (1945). *The Native Culture of the Mariana Islands*. Bishop Museum, Honolulu, Bulletin No. 185.

Thompson, Laura (1947). *Guam and its People,* 3rd ed. Princeton, N.J.: Princeton University Press.

Tobin, J.A. (1953). "An investigation of the socio-political schism on Majuro atoll." Mimeo. Majuro.

Tobin, J.A. (1954). "Ebeye village: an atypical Marshallese community." Mimeo. Majuro.

Tobin, J.A. (1958). "Land tenure in the Marshall Islands." In John de Young, Ed., *Land Tenure Patterns, Trust Territory of the Pacific Islands*, pp. 1-76. Guam: Trust Territory Government.

Tobin, J.A. (1967). *The Resettlement of the Enewetak People*. Unpublished Ph.D. thesis, University of California, Berkeley.

Underwood, J. Hainline (1969). "Preliminary investigations of demographic features and ecological variables of a Micronesian island population." *Micronesica*, 5: 1-24.

United Nations (1954). "Islanders appeal to the United Nations on bomb tests in Pacific Trust area." *United Nations Review*, 1(3): 14-16.

United States Commercial Company (1946). *An Economic Survey of Micronesia*. Mimeo. U.S. Navy.

Useem, John (1945). "Changing structure of a Micronesian society." *American Anthropologist*, 47: 567-588.

Useem, John (1949). *Report on Palau*. Washington, D.C.: Pacific Science Board. Coordinated Investigation of Micronesian Anthropology No. 21.

Useem, John (1950). "Structure of power in Palau." *Social Forces,* 29: 141-148.

Utinomi, H. (1952). *Bibliography of Micronesia*, transl. and rev. O.A. Bushnell et al. Honolulu: University of Hawaii Press.

Viviani, Nancy (1970). *Nauru: Phosphate and Political Progress*. Honolulu: University Press of Hawaii.

Walleser, Sixtus (1913). "Religious beliefs and practices of the inhabitants of Yap," transl. Micronesian Seminar. *Anthropos,* 8: 607-629, 1044-1068.

Weckler, J.E. (1953). "Adoption on Mokil." *American Anthropologist*, 55: 555-568.

Wedgwood, Camilla H. (1936). "Report on research work in Nauru Island, Central Pacific." *Oceania*, 6: 359-391; 7: 1-33.

Wedgwood, Camilla H. (1942/3). "Notes on the Marshall Islands." *Oceania*, 13: 1-23.

Wenkam, Robert and Byron Baker (1971). *Micronesia: The Breadfruit Revolution*. Honolulu: East-West Center Press.

Wiens, H.J. (1962). *Atoll Environment and Ecology*. New Haven, Conn.: Yale University Press.

Wilson, Walter Scott (1968). *Land, Activity and Social Organization of Lelu, Kusaie*. Unpublished Ph.D. thesis, University of Pennsylvania.

Yanaihara, Tadao (1940). *Pacific Islands under Japanese Mandate*. New York: Oxford University Press, Institute of Pacific Relations. (Japanese edition, Tokyo, 1935.)

Index

9